IF YOU LIKE

LED ZEPPELIN...

HERE ARE OVER 200 BANDS, FILMS, RECORDS, AND OTHER ODDITIES THAT YOU WILL LOVE

DAVE THOMPSON

Backbeat Books

AN IMPRINT OF HAL LEONARD CORPORATION

Published in 2012 by Backbeat Books
An Imprint of Hal Leonard Corporation
7777 West Bluemound Road
Milwaukee, WI 53213

Trade Book Division Editorial Offices
33 Plymouth St., Montclair, NJ 07042

Book design by Michael Kellner

Printed in the United States of America

Library of Congress Cataloging-in-Publication Data

Thompson, Dave, 1960 Jan. 3-
    If you like Led Zeppelin : here are over 200 bands, films, records, and other oddities that you will love / Dave Thompson.
        p. cm.
    Includes bibliographical references and index.
    ISBN 978-1-61713-085-4 (alk. paper)
    1. Led Zeppelin (Musical group) 2. Rock musicians--England. 3. Rock music--History and criticism. I. Title.
    ML421.L4T56 2012
    781.66--dc23
                                2012027378

www.backbeatbooks.com

IF YOU LIKE
LIKE
LED ZEPPELIN...

CONTENTS

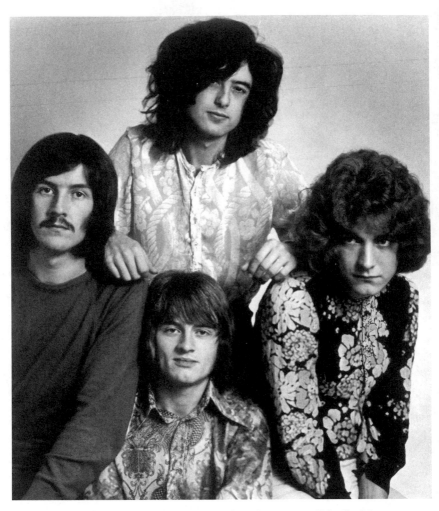

Led Zeppelin, circa 1969. Clockwise from front center: John Paul Jones, John Bonham, Jimmy Page, and Robert Plant. (Photofest)

Introduction

CANDY STORE ROCK

To rock fans of a certain age, there are certain intros that need no further introduction.

Der-neh-der-neh-NEH (der-der-dum der-der-dum)

Ner-ner-ner-ner-ner-ner-ner-ner—DEH-DEH-DEH

De-de-de de-dii-de-de...

Okay, that last one's trickier. But if you got even one out of the three, chances are you could attempt to phoneticize a whole bunch more, and gaze in pitying astonishment at anyone who wasn't as instantly au fait as you are.

Aaaaah-ehhhh-aaaaaaaaaaa—UH!

Across a lifetime that spanned thirteen years, nine LPs, one double live set, and a posthumous compilation, and which has only sporadically been added to since then, Led Zeppelin recorded and released just eighty-five songs. Yet those eighty-five not only set the bar for every rock band of their generation, they became the benchmark for every band that followed.

Between the fall of 1968, when they arose from the ashes of the Yardbirds and taped their first album in a matter of days, and September 1980, when the death of drummer John Bonham rang down the curtain on their career, Led Zeppelin did not simply establish themselves as the biggest rock band in the world. They grasped that throne for all time, because, no matter how successful the groups of the past three decades have been—no matter how readily the financial, attendance, and sales records Zeppelin once set might be smashed—not one of those record-breakers has even threatened to match the sheer weight of influence that Bonham, Jimmy Page, Robert Plant, and John Paul Jones exerted on their surroundings.

No, Bono, not even you.

This is not the place to ponder the reasons why; to analyze the fortuitous confluence of musical streams and strains that Zeppelin, alone of the massive pack plowing the fertile valleys of late-sixties rock, was able to seize upon; to consider the sheer bravado with which manager Peter Grant set about building the legend of a band that wasn't simply untried, but completely unknown; or to pick apart the monstrous marketing machine that allowed Zeppelin to crush all opposition and reinvent rock in their own image.

The fact is, they achieved it and, even more remarkably, they did so by eschewing almost every one of the shortcuts other bands have relied upon. For as long as there had been rock 'n' roll, a hit single was the way to break into the mainstream, and even those late-sixties rockers who claimed to despise the things were not immune to the advantages a smash 45 could bring. Vanilla Fudge, Black Sabbath, Deep Purple, Emerson, Lake & Palmer, Yes, Hawkwind, Argent, bands whose very raison d'être was built around the long-playing statement—they all scored hit singles, and their profiles rose accordingly.

Not Led Zeppelin. Throughout most of the world, they did not even issue singles and, while their American label, Atlantic, did insist on sneaking the 45s out (and scored hits with them), they did so in the knowledge that the band would not be promoting them.

Because that was the other shortcut Led Zeppelin avoided. They would not appear on television, not after a handful of performances early on in their career left the musicians bored and frustrated with the demands of the medium. Led Zeppelin was a live band; therefore, Led Zeppelin would play live. And if you wanted to see them, you had to catch them live as well.

And there's more. Throughout the sixties and seventies, the primary conduit between artist and fan was the music press, a printed medium that devoured several rain forests' worth of trees every month to fill the average fan's appetite for hot news and info. In Zeppelin's British homeland through much of that period, there were no fewer than five music papers appearing every week (*Melody Maker*, *New Musical Express*, *Sounds*, and *Record Mirror*, plus shorter-lived enterprises like *Disc* and the appallingly titled *National Rock Star*). There was the biweekly *Street Life* and a slew of monthlies too. Plus an ever-changing roster of magazines dedicated to the teenybop market.

The United States had less to choose from, but the best of the bunch remain legends to this day—*Creem*, *Circus*, *Rolling Stone* (in the days when its music coverage came first and was generally better than anyone else's). All sold by the bucket-load, all were savagely independent, and all were essential reading. A front-page story in any one of those was worth a gold disc before the new album was even released.

Led Zeppelin ignored them. Not completely, and certainly not exclusively. But interviews with the band were nevertheless at a premium, as manager Peter Grant laid out an unspoken dictate that flew in the face of all commercial common sense. Yes, you could talk *about* the band as much as you liked. But you'd be very, very lucky if you got to talk *to* them.

Any one of these dictates could easily have backfired. The press could have turned against the band, the record buyers could have shrugged with disinterest, the couch potatoes could have remained on the couch.

But they didn't, because Led Zeppelin had one thing no other band of the age could come close to possessing. It was called mystique, and that is so unquantifiable that, again, we will not even try. Put simply, however, people *trusted* Led Zeppelin.

Trusted them to make a great album without wanting to hear a three-minute snippet before they laid down their cash.

Trusted them to put on a great show, without needing to catch a sanitized highlight on *American Bandstand*.

And trusted them to have something to say, without having to wade through three thousand words of edited conversation in search of John Bonham's thoughts on the Nixon administration.

But there was something else that made Led Zeppelin special, that raised them above the hue and cry of the rest of the rock pack, and established them on a musical plateau that—again—has never been scaled by anyone else. And that was their openness to influence, their willingness to listen, and their ability to seamlessly assimilate so many personal fascinations into what became a very public whole.

That is what this book is about. Not the story of Led Zeppelin as it ran from day to day, because that has been done on so many occasions (an annotated bibliography of the best of those books can be found among this volume's appendices), but the story as it drew from and, in turn, spread out to the rest of the musical world.

Not every recommendation in these pages will be to every fan's taste, and not every assumption drawn from the available evidence will be agreeable to all. But with over two hundred fresh artists, albums, genres, and songs for the reader to investigate, the chances are good you will like most of them.

And why? Because you already like Led Zeppelin.

AUTHOR'S NOTE

Throughout this book, certain names, titles, etc., have been listed in boldface. This occurs only at the first, or primary, reference to each item, and it is done to indicate that the name or title is considered worthy of your further inspection.

NOTE ON SOURCES

Unless explicitly credited in the text, all quoted material in this book is drawn from my own interviews with the named subjects.

Cream. (Photofest)

1

WHERE WERE YOU IN '68?:
THE BIRTH OF A BAND OR THREE

It was the year in which Led Zeppelin was born; and, perhaps more than any other in rock history, it was the year in which the future was cast. It was the morning after the very long night before—the year, the history books insist, in which rock 'n' roll lost the innocence it had only just regained the previous summer. It was the year in which the double album came of age, and politics carved their presence into the grooves. It was the year when the first supergroups arose from the egalitarianism of the past, and profits first became a paramount concern. But most of all, it was the year in which rock realized that everything it had accomplished in the past was simply a rehearsal. 1968 was the year in which things turned serious.

The previous twelve months had seen record sales in America reach an all-time high. With more than $1 billion worth of music shifted in just 365 days, record industry profits had more than doubled in a decade.

For the first time, also, LP sales were outstripping singles, and that too made an impact. It would be misleading to say it was high finance alone that pushed so many bands into new realms of musical seriousness. The ambitious pastures opened up by **the Beatles'** ***Sgt. Pepper's Lonely Hearts Club Band*** accomplished that, and the artists who followed its lead did so for artistic reasons. But record companies were another matter entirely. They scented big bucks and they wanted them, and the notion that the youth of America suddenly had previously untold sums of disposable cash to flash and splash on their hairy rock idols was not something that could be easily ignored.

Bands, too, understood their audience wanted something more than the lightweight two- or three-minute ditties that had sustained their careers until now. In 1967, many ... too many, in fact ... had looked towards literature and fantasy for inspiration, and turned out some remarkable music in the process. But the real world was not like that. It was not peopled with hobbits and goblins and rainbow-riding unicorns. It was a place where bloodshed was commonplace and death was too easy, and rioting was the only means by which a raised voice could be guaranteed a hearing.

A nation founded upon the principles of freedom was suddenly being ruled by fear, at least if you were young and long-haired. Like a wounded animal lashing out at anything it didn't (or didn't want to) understand, society was both indiscriminate about its targets and insensitive to its hypocrisy.

Today, critics of the government's often heavy-handed response to Internet misbehavior complain of an establishment that has lost all sense of context and irony, citing (among so many examples) the British tourist turned back from LAX in early 2012 after tweeting to his friends that he was coming to "destroy America." But, really, it is only the language of misunderstanding that has changed, not the misunderstanding itself. One generation's commonplace slang has always been another's murderous threat.

Hippie was a dirty word; *student*, *pacifist*, and *protester* likewise. Visiting California the previous year, the English band **Cream** had expressed astonishment at the freedom that seemed to permeate the very streets. True, not every passing cop was willing to look the other way when he stumbled on a gang of kids taking a crafty toke, but he wasn't about to start cracking skulls with his nightstick, either.

Overnight, all that had changed, and rock 'n' roll would soundtrack it all.

From **the Rolling Stones**' "Street Fighting Man" to the Beatles' "Revolution," from **Eric Burdon and the Animals**' "Sky Pilot" to the Lettermen's "All the Grey Haired Men," voices were raised in opposition to everything the authorities were bringing to bear. **The Jimi Hendrix Experience** grasped **Bob Dylan**'s "All Along the Watchtower" before most people had even heard the album from which it came (*John Wesley Harding*) and electrified sentiments that might have seemed mere allegory in Dylan's hands, but which became a mantra among American troops fighting in Vietnam: "There must be some way out of here!"

The Stones, in particular, came out fighting. Scrambling to make up the ground (both musical and critical) they'd lost with the psychedelic stew of *Their Satanic Majesties Request* the previous year, they hooked up with producer Jimmy Miller to craft an album that would both reconfirm the band's blues traditions and dismiss their (and everybody else's) psychedelic meanderings as simply a passing aberration. And they succeeded with an album that not only reaffirmed the Stones' roots, but reinvented them.

The ten songs that made up ***Beggars Banquet*** fit the band like a glove. Nobody ever believed the group had traveled two thousand light-years from home or spent a night in another land. But the brute-force sexuality of "Stray Cat Blues" and the badlands hoedown of "Prodigal Son" merged so perfectly with the Stones' public persona that their imagery became utterly inseparable from the performers, a process that reached its terrifying apogee with **"Sympathy for the Devil,"** a lyric Mick Jagger wrote after reading banned Soviet author Mikhail Bulgakov's *The Master and Margarita*, but which was far easier to view as unadorned autobiography. Even today, as many legends and myths adhere to "Sympathy for the Devil" as the rest of the band's output put together.

"Sympathy for the Devil" dominates *Beggars Banquet*, but by no means does it outclass it. The scratchy lilt of "No Expectations," the country pastiche "Dear Doctor," the chugging blues of "Parachute Woman"—with every passing number, the aura of menace builds and builds, until the valedictory "Salt of the Earth" croaks it to a close that is all the more haunting for its lack of the expected climax. *Beggars Banquet* sounds like it wanted to end with an apocalypse. Instead, it leaves you hanging on the brink, wondering what could ever, possibly, follow it up.

The Stones manufactured their menace. Other songs took on their own foreboding meaning, whether they were intended to or not. Who, among those who were alive and thinking in 1968, can listen to Mary Hopkins's "Those Were the Days"—one of the biggest hits of the entire year—without translating the song's eerie edge of sad nostalgia into a lament for the life we led before all hell broke loose at home and abroad?

Elsewhere, the emergence of the first proto-metal bands, **the Jeff Beck Group** and **Blue Cheer** among them, might not have posited a formal protest against the political machine that was crushing hope and extinguishing promise, but it was a protest nonetheless, the realization that if you turned up the volume loud enough, you might just be able to drown out the screams.

It was no coincidence that, even as **the Who** worked up what would become *Tommy* (the archetypal story of the blind leading the bland), they were also rehearsing a live set that kicked back into rock's more innocent past, resurrecting **Eddie Cochran**'s "Summertime Blues" and **Mose Allison**'s "Young Man Blues," and reinventing them as virtual talismans, reminders again of happier days twisted through the prism of irony. With the military draft growing louder every day, how wonderful it must have been when your biggest worry was whether or not you'd be able to borrow the car for the evening.

"1968 was a funny old year," the Hendrix Experience's Noel Redding once recalled. "When we were out on the road, you could see that people were scared, they were looking out at the world and everything they'd been brought up to believe, and everything they thought they were creating in 1967, was falling apart around their ears. We were insulated from a lot of it, we'd play a town, then move on, but you'd talk to kids and a few months later, reading the paper and looking at the casualty figures, you'd wonder, how many of them had you talked to somewhere a few months earlier? And now they were dead or injured, fighting a war that very few of them seemed to believe in, or even understand."

You could almost hear Arlo Guthrie strike up the opening patterns of "Alice's Restaurant" as Redding spoke.

But the war was only one part of the equation that appeared to be painting the collapse of civilization in sky-high neon lettering. The assassination of Martin Luther King on April 4 was followed two months later by the killing of Democratic front-runner Bobby Kennedy, and both carved their own bloodied initials into society's flesh, twin outrages that pulled the rug out from beneath anybody who felt America (and, therefore, much of the world) still had a hope of surviving the decade.

It would be so misleading, however, to recall 1968 as a year dominated by protest and riot. True, the all-pervading image of the **MC5**, kicking out the jams at the head of the Detroit underground, is a difficult one to shake free of, and it certainly cannot be divorced from any discussion of the year. But the MC5 were little more than a local cult at that time, destined for infamy more through their associations with radical kingpin John Sinclair, and their unequivocal refusal to tone down the language on their *Kick Out the Jams* debut album. To America and the rock world at large, 1968 was the year of a series of triumphs that could scarcely have been further removed from the political tumult if they'd tried.

Cream, after all, was one of the most apolitical bands you could hope to find, at least in a major rock arena, yet they were also one of the biggest in the land; and their contribution to the unfolding year, **Wheels of Fire**, was gargantuan as well. A double set, half of this eye-catching new package drew from the studio recordings Cream had spent the last year working on. The remainder was be boiled down from live shows recorded earlier in the year, because it was onstage that Cream's brilliance was at its most vivacious.

A brilliant album, a stunning achievement, a Herculean melding of craft and creativity, the centerpiece of *Wheels of Fire* was the dichotomy that dogged Cream throughout their career: the uneasy marriage of, on the studio disc, a succession of sharp, tight rock songs and, on the other, four sprawling jams.

To modern ears, accustomed as they are to the "legend" of Cream, the two faces are not so extreme. Journeying through the strangely **Yardbirds**-y "Passing Time," the haunted neo-orchestrations of "As You Said," the lumbering "Politician," and the eerie "Deserted Cities of the Heart," we can slip from the whimsy of the studio record's "Pressed Rat and Warthog" to the thunder of the in-concert "Toad" and easily understand how the same man (drummer Ginger Baker) wrote them both.

At the time, however, they were as divisive as any other facet of the group. Reiterating the complaints it had slung at Cream's last album, **Disraeli Gears**, *Rolling Stone* opened its review of the album with the admonishment, "Cream is good at a number of things; unfortunately song-writing and recording are not among them. *Disraeli Gears* was far better." The live record, on the other hand, was the food of the gods. Preaching at a time when the vast majority of live albums were little more than contractual obligations, poorly recorded and even harder to listen to, the review insisted, "this is the kind of thing that people who have seen Cream perform walk away raving about, and it's good to, at last, have it on a record." Such enthusiasm still holds true. In 2003, *Classic Rock* magazine published its critics' choices of the Top 50 live albums ever released. *Wheels of Fire* came in at #50.

But still, the divide between the two discs was disconcerting. The band's U.K. label, Polydor, was so nervous about the LP's schizophrenia that the scheduled double album was also released as two individual discs (the snappy *In the Studio* in August, and the lumbering *Live at the Fillmore* in December), so that fans of one would not perforcedly be saddled with an unwanted other. Neither was it a wasted gesture. While the full-weight *Wheels of Fire* marched to #3 on the U.K. chart, the slimmed-down *In the Studio* soared almost as high, to #7. *Live at the Fillmore*, on the other hand, did not even make the listings.

The record was even bigger in America. The most eagerly awaited new release of a summer that was already girding for fresh albums from the Grateful Dead, **Jefferson Airplane** and **the Vanilla Fudge**, *Wheels of Fire* was released in the United States in July, and marched straight to the top of the chart, bumping brass man Herb Alpert out of the way in the process. It remained there for a month, until the latest by the Doors came to push it off its perch, but it was still in the album chart close to one year later.

From the commercially sublime to the disastrously ridiculous: **The Kinks'** *Village Green Preservation Society* scarcely sold a bean upon release, although it has long since ascended to those rarefied strata of albums that (say it softly) are now widely proclaimed to be "better than *Pepper*." That's a yardstick that may only be worth the weight of whichever critic holds it, but still it has ensured the immortality of a record even Ray Davies described as "the most successful failure of all time." Successful in that the album said everything he wanted it to; "failure" in that ...well, in that it barely sold a bean on release.

The people who always loved the album, of course, will always love it and for good reason. From the hymnal title track through to the heart-tearing nostalgia of "Village Green" itself, from the scatty whimsy of "Phenomenal Cat" to the fiendish fairy-tailoring of "Wicked Annabella," *Village Green Preservation Society* is the childhood memory you recall but cannot quite grasp, the favorite TV episode that never turns up in the reruns, the old lover whose photo was eaten by the cat. It is certainly the Kinks' greatest album, and one of the decade's finest as well. 1968 would have been a lot poorer without it.

Valuable too is **Pink Floyd**'s *A Saucerful of Secrets*, an album of cosmic rumination and painstaking improvisation that sought only to prove its makers could survive life without frontman and songwriter Syd Barrett, but wound up creating far more than that. The title track alone remains one of the most pivotal numbers in the Pink Floyd catalog, *not* for what it is, but for what it represented; as guitarist David Gilmour later pointed out, it set the stage for so much of what Floyd would accomplish in the years to come, while bandmate Roger Waters confirmed that "it was the first thing we'd done without Syd that we thought was any good." Their adhesion to those principles over the next five years would ultimately birth *The Dark Side of the Moon*.

What is interesting, however, as we filter through what are today adjudged some of the year's most significant releases, is that few of them were especially huge hits. The Zombies' purposefully misspelt *Odessey and Oracle* barely scratched the Top 100, and who among us paid any attention to such delights as the pioneering fusion of **Julie Driscoll and Brian Auger and the Trinity**'s *Open*? The eponymous debut by **the Crazy World of Arthur Brown** made #7 on the strength of the all-consuming "Fire," but **the Small Faces**' *Ogdens' Nut Gone Flake* climbed no higher than #159 in America, even as it topped the U.K. chart.

The re-formed **Byrds** had already run out of feathers, as *The Notorious Byrd Brothers* flapped around the lower reaches of the Top 50; the much-vaunted Moby Grape were already in decline; and, though the Mothers of Invention certainly scored their biggest hit yet with *We're Only in It for the Money*, a week at #30 was scarcely going to dent the big boys...especially when Frank Zappa's second album of the year, the delightful *Lumpy Gravy*, foundered a full 129 places lower down.

And so on.

Of course, one can never judge an act's importance by its popularity, as a swift glance at a list of the year's #1 albums will prove. In the United Kingdom, balladeers Andy Williams, Val Doonican, and the perennial soundtrack to *The Sound of Music* did battle with the expected Beatles (but *not* the Stones), the Small Faces and Scott Walker, the Hollies and Tom Jones, and, reflecting the U.K.'s long-standing love affair with soul music, hit collections by the Supremes and the Four Tops, and the recently deceased Otis Redding.

In the United States, the picture was no less distorted. The Beatles bookended the year's chart-toppers with *Magical Mystery Tour* and the double **"White Album,"** while new offerings by Simon & Garfunkel, the Rascals, **Janis Joplin with Big Brother and the Holding Company**, the Jimi Hendrix Experience and **the Doors** pointed to the strength of the relatively recently launched FM radio boom. But such a triumph for sensible listening is balanced by the three months at the top that were divided between Paul Mauriat & His Orchestra (purveyors of the lush instrumental hit "Love Is Blue"), country singer Glen Campbell, and the jumping rhythms of Herb Alpert & the Tijuana Brass.

The singles chart offers an even more bizarre barometer.

American chart-toppers in 1968 included John Fred and His Playboy Band's stupendously original "Judy in Disguise (with Glasses)," Jeannie C. Riley's "Harper Valley PTA," and Bobby Goldsboro's snuff-rock epic "Honey." And bubbling behind them, taking the charts by storm almost every time they released another 45, the arch bubblegum factory of Kasenetz-Katz was peaking so high in 1968, it seemed unlikely they would ever come down again.

But it was also the year when the Jeff Beck Group uncorked **Truth** and singlehandedly served up the blueprint that would create Led Zeppelin. Beck remembers the day he sat listening to a white label of Zeppelin's year-end debut album with Jimmy Page. Page was so proud of that record, and Beck agreed that he ought to be—at least until the needle hit the third track on side one, and "You Shook Me" shook out of the speakers. The same "You Shook Me" that Beck had included on *Truth*; the same "You Shook Me" that a passing John Paul Jones had gifted with an immortal organ line. "I looked at him and said, 'Jim ...what?' and the tears were coming out with anger. I thought, 'This is a piss take, it's got to be.' I mean, there was *Truth* still spinning on everybody's turntable ... Then I realized it was serious."

It is probably no more accurate to say that, without *Truth*, there would have been no *Led Zeppelin I*, than it is to argue that, without the Velvet Underground (whose *White Light/White Heat* sank without trace this same year) there would have been no David Bowie.

But without the Beck Group to pave the way, Zeppelin would certainly have found their own elevation a little harder to pull off, and without the rest of 1968, the seeds that brought to such strident life by that opening metallic guitar choke may never have taken root. 1968 was the year of many things. But if any one phrase sums it up, it was the year of the Communication Breakdown.

Albert King, in 1972. (Columbia Pictures/Photofest)

2

WE'RE GONNA GROOVE:
THE STORY OF THE BLUES

Led Zeppelin emerged during what music history refers to as the British Blues Explosion, the same end-of-the-sixties upheaval that spawned such future fellow giants as **Ten Years After**, **Peter Green's Fleetwood Mac**, **Free**, and the Jeff Beck Group.

It is generally regarded as a short-lived movement, for all the influence it would have on the rock scene of the next decade. Fleetwood Mac alone would truly survive, but only after morphing into an AOR hit machine, while the rest would largely be crushed beneath the cacophonous assault of ever-louder riffs, ever-more lurching shuffles, and a general obsession with the mutant history now calls heavy metal.

In reality, however, the events of the late 1960s were simply the culmination of a musical interlude that commenced a full ten years earlier, in the late 1950s, as a generation of what we now call the first baby boomers flocked to embrace the exciting sounds flooding into the country from the great ports of Liverpool, Southampton, and, of course, London, and which themselves traced their genesis back to turn-of-the-century America.

Merchant seamen returning from the United States were importing the music they heard and purchased while they were there, and future Beatle John Lennon was just one of myriad entranced teenagers who would wait at dockside to hear, or hear about, the 45s and LPs the latest new arrival came home with.

A grapevine developed, secret whispers of hot new recordings that passed from acolyte to acolyte before washing up in the presence of someone who had actually heard, or better still possessed, the record in question. The more adventurous souls started writing to the addresses on the back of every release and purchasing music direct from the source. Specialist record stores began carrying the latest, greatest sounds. And musicians started learning the songs, some with the studious air of anthropologists aiming for nothing less than absolute authenticity, others with a more devil-may-care approach, capturing in sound the nuclear fission they felt in their hearts when they heard these strange songs.

Strange, because what could the American blues, and the experiences of the American bluesmen who wrote them, possibly have in common with the life of a suburban teenager in late-1950s/early-1960s England? There were no sharecroppers in Shoreditch, no chain gangs in Chelmsford, and the Thames Estuary made a poor replacement for the Mississippi Delta. A good American blues embraced life, death, and despair, a few dead dogs, and a mean-hearted woman. A good English blues might begin with missing the bus to work, sulk about being ignored by a spotty girl named Tracy, and wind up lamenting being late for the first five minutes of a favorite television program.

But the songs translated anyway, not through words but through emotions, not through lyrics but through feel. In the same way that the first (and near-simultaneous) burst of rock 'n' roll shook, rattled, and rolled its audience with little more than lyrical nonsense and frenetic shouting, so the blues captured an experience that was so quintessentially human it did not need to be literal. The songs that made the greatest impact on the British music scene were those that translated into the local dialect without actually meaning a thing.

"The whole thing was, you had to have a broken heart," Fleetwood Mac's **Peter Green** explained. "Or something not quite broken, so you could express it in music."

Anthropology became archaeology. Without even realizing what they were searching for, young blues hunters set about digging deep into the American record company catalogs in search of ever-more wonderful buried treasure. Sometimes they sought out earlier versions of the songs already regarded as blues classics, in the hope of discovering a lost nuance or missing verse with which to astound and astonish their audience. Other times, an unfamiliar name might catch the attention, a bluesman whom positively nobody else had ever heard of. Every fan had his own passion, and every bluesman was ripe for rediscovery.

"I still crave those little bits of unreleased stuff," Green continued. "I have records [by] Elmore James which have a lot of unreleased takes, false takes, all that. If you love someone, you love to hear things like that, the false takes."

Here's a frightening thought. The blues of the 1900s were no more distant to the fans of the earliest sixties than the sixties themselves are from today. In 2012, we celebrate the fiftieth anniversary of the first Beatles single. In 1962, the Beatles might have celebrated the same anniversary for Hart Wands's "Dallas Blues," the first song ever copyrighted with the word *blues* (as a mood, as opposed to a color) in its title.

But it was a different world all the same, a world without any of the advantages (or, at least, technological time-savers) we take for granted today. Forget there being no Internet; there were scarcely any telephones, let alone radio or television. A record born in New Orleans might live and die there as well, without any hope of being heard anyplace else, because how was it going to travel? Maybe a visitor would take a copy home, maybe someone would hear it and sing it someplace else. But there was no FM DJ to blast it across the state line, no record company distributor whose reach extended from coast to coast. Word of mouth was the only advertising—that, and any given performer's ability to travel north or south in search of a new gig.

Yet the blues flourished, even if the bluesmen themselves remained largely starving. A song might be sold to a well-heeled music industry man and become a standard in someone else's repertoire (the concept of paying honestly accounted royalties was even less developed than it is today) and, by the 1920s, 1930s at the latest, the blues was established as America's soul.

In the most general terms, two distinct branches of the blues grew up, named for the areas in which their creators seemed centered:

Chicago, for the industrial North; Delta, for the rural South. Other specifically named breeds flourished, of course—things like Piedmont blues and jump blues—but one referred primarily to a guitar picking style, and the other to an up-tempo, horn-driven style that owed a lot to swing. Today you can catch the **Carolina Chocolate Drops** for a modern approximation of those hybrids (and much more besides). Half a century ago, though, if you wanted the real thing, the "I woke up one morning" mourning, you went for the Delta or Chicago, and they packed traditions that predated "Dallas Blues" by anything up to a century, back to the slave-era spirituals that morphed into cleverly masked social comment in a world where newspapers rarely questioned the status quo, and most of the questioners were unable to read anyway.

There were no stars, not in the manner we imagine today. The United States was pocked with tiny record labels, some existing for no more than a record or two, that would record whoever wandered into the studio and pump out fragile shellac 78s that may or may not have survived the passing of time. There are still artists from the 1920s and 1930s whose best work survives only in the imagination of collectors, because the records simply don't exist any longer. There are others whose art is known from just one or two copies of a worn-out 78, and while CDs and the Internet have both allowed that art to reach a wider audience, still there's a world out there our ears might never explore.

That was the world the first British blues bands wanted to open up. **Alexis Korner**, **Cyril Davies**, and **John Mayall** are legendary names in the world of British blues, founders of pioneering blues bands whose ranks would open up to birth the names that led the music to glory. Jack Bruce, Ginger Baker, Mick Jagger, Charlie Watts, Rod Stewart, Peter Green, Mick Taylor—a sprawling family tree of early-sixties British blues musicians can trace back to that trio in nine cases out of ten, with the tenth probably having a loose connection as well.

Yet the names would have been worthless without the music, and the music was as timeless as the careers it would help create. When Led Zeppelin played their first concerts in late 1968, and recorded their debut LP soon after, their repertoire was as fresh as tomorrow, but it was also as familiar as your very own face. And the writers their ears fell upon form an exquisitely exclusive library of bluesmen that itself tells the story of the blues, in all its heartbroken, hard-living, and harmonious glory.

Philadelphia soul and bluesman **Garnet Mimms**'s "As Long as I Have You" was among the songs jammed into Led Zeppelin's very first live show, in Gladsaxe, Denmark, on September 7, 1968—when the band was still billed as the New Yardbirds, and included that band's "For Your Love" in their set.

It was not, as the blues went, an especially ancient song. Born in 1933, Mimms had only been recording since 1953, when the West Virginia native cut his first few records with a gospel group. A decade later, however, he was recording with songwriter **Bert Berns**—the man whose own legacy includes writing **"Here Comes the Night,"** "Twist and Shout," and "Hang On Sloopy"—and a chain of U.S. hit singles swiftly followed. "As Long as I Have You" was not among them, but its place in Led Zeppelin's early lore ensures that many Mimms compilations tuck it on board.

Berns's own "Baby Come On Home" was another primal Led Zeppelin favorite, while their early fascination with **Ben E. King**'s "We're Gonna Groove" saw that latter song even make it onto 1982's odds-and-sods collection *Coda*, alongside a clutch of other outtakes and off-cuts. The Berns song, meanwhile, made it onto the band's 1993 compilation. Back at the beginning, however, the two tunes were simply fresh ideas for the future, sharing headspace with what would become the soul of the band's debut LP, and some of the most spellbinding blues in Zeppelin's career.

WILLIE DIXON: HE SHOOK THEM

Willie Dixon's "You Shook Me" is the first bona fide blues on *Led Zeppelin I*; and his "I Can't Quit You Baby" is the second. A couple of out-of-court settlements in years to come would see his name added to the credits to both "Whole Lotta Love" and "Bring It On Home," and extend his influence onto *Led Zeppelin II.* The rights and wrongs of that latter credit, incidentally, still exercise Jimmy Page today—the song was actually intended as a tribute to **Sonny Boy Williamson II**, a bluesman with whom Page had recorded in England in 1965, and who in turn recorded the definitive version of the Dixon song of the same name. A tiny fragment of the original is all anyone could claim had been borrowed, but fragments were all the lawyers needed.

Nevertheless, all are an indication of just how highly Page and his bandmates rated the Vicksburg, Mississippi–born bluesman, and they were not alone. A romp through Dixon's recording career turns up some of the most familiar blues songs of them all: **"Little Red Rooster"** became a huge hit for the Rolling Stones; "Spoonful" was a staple of Cream's repertoire; **"Back Door Man"** was a major part of the early Doors mythology; **"I Ain't Superstitious"** was a peak of the Jeff Beck Group's *Truth*; **"I Just Want to Make Love to You," "Wang Dang Doodle," "Evil," "Hoochie Coochie Man"**—the list goes on.

A former professional boxer who did not turn seriously to music until he was into his mid-twenties, and already in his mid-forties when his songs first started attracting British ears, Dixon was quick to make his mark on the Chicago blues scene.

Cutting his greatest records, inevitably, for the legendary Chess label, Dixon saw his compositions covered by **Muddy Waters** and **Howlin' Wolf**; recorded with **Bo Diddley** and **Chuck Berry**; and was so much a part of the musical landscape that Jimi Hendrix, the Allman Brothers, and the Grateful Dead would all look toward his songbook for material. By the time Dixon died in 1992, he had entered both the Blues Hall of Fame and the Blues Foundation, and won a Grammy for his 1989 album *Hidden Charms*.

Less feted on the first Led Zeppelin LP, but an integral part of its epic finale, is a song immortalized by another blues legend, **Albert King**, but written by Stax Records house band Booker T. and the M.G.'s. "The Hunter" was a recent addition to King's catalog; he cut it in 1967, but it immediately moved into Ike and Tina Turner's repertoire, and also into that of the then-fledgling British blues band Free.

Zeppelin took it too, jamming their own interpretation of Howlin' Wolf's "How Many More Years" one night in the studio (it became "How Many More Times" in their hands), and then slipping almost unintentionally into a few lines of "The Hunter," for a magnificent performance that more than any on that debut LP exemplifies just what astonishing musicians the quartet were. No instrument outplays any other, no ingredient is less focused than another, but whatever player you choose to lock your hearing onto suddenly seems to be giving his greatest performance ever. For some ears, it is Robert Plant's so-intuitive vocal; for others, it is the gymnastics turned by both Page and Jones. But for others, it is Bonham's drums that raise "The Hunter" to glory, chasing the melody with such deliberate strength that the song still ranked among his very finest outings by the time the band came to an end. No, it isn't "Moby Dick," but somehow it didn't need to be.

And if the studio version was remarkable, in concert the jam took on even more epic proportions, as **John Lee Hooker**'s "Boogie Chillun" was also wont to materialize, together with Arthur "Big Boy" Crudup's **Elvis Presley** hit "That's Alright Mama."

Howlin' Wolf's influence resurfaces on "The Lemon Song," the crudest slice of sexual innuendo in Led Zeppelin's catalog, but also a solid appreciation of the often dramatically sexual content of early blues. Wolf's "Killing Floor," a live favorite throughout Zeppelin's early U.S. tours, would become the basis of the song, although it would be 1972 before a legal challenge saw Wolf's name added to the song's writing credits.

There could be room for more. Another live favorite from Zeppelin's early years, whose ghost certainly dances in "The Lemon Song," was "Travelling Riverside Blues," as written and recorded by possibly the greatest bluesman of them all, **Robert Johnson**. It would be 1990 before Led Zeppelin would allow their own formative stab at the song to see release (although, as with every other song discussed in this book, the bootleggers had got to it long, long before), but Page and Plant in particular would never let the opportunity to praise Johnson pass them by.

In truth, Johnson's claim to greatness arguably lies as much in his early death, and abbreviated career, as it does in the sheer quality of the few recordings he left behind, while the legend of him selling his soul to the Devil in exchange for mastering his music lies at the heart of every great blues legend.

Born in 1911, and dead at twenty-seven, Johnson wasn't the first person to have made that particular exchange, not even in the annals of the blues. **Clara Smith** was singing "Done Sold My Soul to the Devil (And My Heart's Done Turned to Stone)" in 1924, almost a decade before Johnson exchanged contracts. And it is also possible he may not have even done it at all. Historian Alan Lomax shrugs the story of Johnson's pact with Lucifer completely to one side, retelling it as merely a distortion of another belief entirely. According to Lomax, every bluesman—in fact, every musician on earth—was destined for an eternity in hell, because playing any but the most sacred of songs was itself an unforgivable sin.

Indeed, even Jimmy Page has his own variation on the legend, courtesy of his oft-mentioned but seldom explained fascination with **Aleister Crowley**, a twentieth-century magician who was as happy being termed "the most wicked man in Britain" by others, as he was describing himself as "the Great Beast."

Journalist Mick Houghton is one of the writers who tried to pin Page down on this subject, in a 1976 interview with *Sounds*. But Page was not playing ball: "I just don't want to go into it too much. I don't want to get like Pete Townsend and Meher Baba because I'm sure most people would find it really boring. I'm not trying to interest anyone in Aleister Crowley any more than I am in Charles Dickens. All it was, was that at a particular time he was expounding self-liberation, which is so important. He was like an eye into the world, into the forthcoming situation.

"My studies have been quite intensive, but I don't particularly want to go into it because it's a personal thing and isn't in relation to anything I do as a musician apart from that I've employed his system in my own day-to-day life."

Of course there are myriad researchers out there in Internetland who will help you pinpoint those precise moments in Zeppelin's discography where Page's passion for music and fascination with Crowley become inextricably aligned (let us not forget that "Stairway to Heaven" is quite the occult masterpiece, albeit one whose lyrics were Robert Plant's concern). But anybody wishing to dig deep into Crowleyana, aside from visiting the vast corpus of books and writings that bear his name, should also check out the two-CD set *Aleister Crowley*, a collection of vintage recordings of the man himself, all delivered in a shakily querulous voice that sounds scarcely more beastly than an old lady buying cat food.

We digress.

Whether it is true or not, Johnson's tale of meeting the Devil at the crossroads, and trading his soul for a guitar that killed, was swift to enter mythology and folklore, and it doesn't matter how good Johnson was on some mythical scale of bluesy greatness. The fact is, the forty-two recordings Johnson cut between 1936 and his murder in Greenwood, Mississippi, on August 13, 1938, include some of the most oft-covered and oft-praised blues songs of them all. "Travelling Riverside Blues" ain't even the greatest of them.

Another Zeppelin favorite was **Bukka White**, an American Delta bluesman who some sources say might have drifted into absolute obscurity had Bob Dylan not seized upon his "Fixin' to Die Blues" early on in his career. Might have, but probably not, because John Mayall was playing White's **"Parchman Farm"** around the U.K. at the same time, and a decade later White was rebirthed when Led Zeppelin not only gnawed his "Shake 'Em On Down" for their third album's "Hats Off to (Roy) Harper," but also stabbed "Fixin' to Die" for a BBC radio broadcast in April 1971.

The "Charles Obscure" who is credited with arranging what the *Led Zeppelin III* album sleeve insists is a traditional song is, of course, Page, while the same debut Dylan album that featured "Fixin' to Die" is also the source for what probably ranks among the most egregious of Zeppelin borrowings: when they lifted "In My Time of Dying" for *Physical Graffiti* and claimed they'd written it themselves.

In fact, it's a traditional gospel song that, occasionally under the title "Jesus Gonna Make Up My Dying Bed," has been around since at least the 1920s. **Blind Willie Johnson**, a self-taught guitarist born in Texas in 1897, and dead by 1945, recorded it in 1927 as his debut single, igniting a career that trod a very skillful line between blues and gospel. It has since been covered by artists as far afield as the Grateful Dead, **the White Stripes**, and Bruce Springsteen. But it is Led Zeppelin whose debt to Johnson's catalog is perhaps the most pronounced (if not paid in full); for not only did they spirit away "In My Time of Dying," they also took elements of his "Nobody's Fault but Mine" for a highlight of their next album, *Presence*.

But back to "In My Time of Dying." Both Charlie Patton and radical folkie Josh White would make their own beds around it over the next decade; madcap English duo John Otway and Wild Willy Barrett were in the habit of performing wildly extended versions based around the Dylan prototype throughout the early 1970s, while former Lovin' Spoonful main man John Sebastian and Dutch rockers Shocking Blue also cut versions before Zeppelin laid their hands on it.

Nevertheless, it was Dylan's 1962 version—"In My Time of Dyin'"—that brought the song most heavily to prominence, as his debut album, ***Bob Dylan***, established itself as essential listening to anyone with even half an ear for folk and Americana.

Within weeks of its release, songs like "Baby, Let Me Follow You Down" and "Man of Constant Sorrow" had become staples of the folk scene on both sides of the Atlantic, while his "House of the Rising Sun" was indirectly responsible for the birth of folk rock, after a Newcastle, England, band called the Animals rearranged the song for electric guitar and organ and topped charts around the world with it.

Led Zeppelin have their own long relationship with both Dylan's debut and its follow-up. In one of the first interviews he ever gave, with *International Times* journalist Mark Williams in April 1969, Robert Plant enthused, "The first music that appealed to me, when I was at school even, was stuff like Dylan's 'Corrina, Corrina' and when you look deeper into that sort of thing you find there's a lot of the same feelings that are in blues music, like Leadbelly's stuff and then you realise that the blues field is a very wide one."

Marianne Faithfull, for whom frequently Page played guitar during the mid-1960s, recorded versions of both "House of the Rising Sun" and *The Freewheelin' Bob Dylan*'s "Blowin' in the Wind," five years before "Fixin' to Die" entered Led Zeppelin's repertoire, and a decade before "In My Time of Dying" was enshrined. In every case, however, though we can admire the prototype, it must be acknowledged that what Led Zeppelin did with the songs was what made them the band they became. For they did not simply cover a song. They redesigned it, jamming it through however-many minutes of often-inspired semi-improvisation (their "In My Time of Dying" is eleven minutes long)—and really, that's what the blues is all about: feelings.

The Delta comes to startling life on Led Zeppelin's fourth album. "When the Levee Breaks" was recorded and written by **Memphis Minnie**, perhaps the greatest female blues singer of them all. Born in 1897, she was already playing nightclubs in her early teens before running away to join the circus. She was thirty-two before she cut her first record, with husband Kansas Joe McCoy. While they would part in 1935, Minnie's recording career would extend over forty years, longer than any other female blues singer of the age.

"When the Levee Breaks" told the tale of the Great Flood of 1927, a Mississippi-wide disaster that followed nine months of unnaturally heavy rains, and inundated Missouri, Illinois, Arkansas, Mississippi, Texas, and Louisiana. Dams and levees were useless. If the river could not crest them, it simply went around them. Water up to thirty feet deep in places covered an area the size of Vermont, New Hampshire, Massachusetts, and Connecticut combined. And the rains kept on pouring.

One hundred forty-five levees gave way; twenty-seven thousand square miles of land were underwater. Up in Memphis, the Mississippi measured sixty miles wide at one point. "When the Levee Breaks," then, is an example of the blues as living history, a function that is often forgotten today. It is a point, too, where the blues intersects with folk music—Jimmy Page's other great musical passion and the source, as their dalliance with Dylan proves, of much of Led Zeppelin's influence, both stated and otherwise.

Returning to *Led Zeppelin I*, Jimmy Page first heard Anne Bredon's "Babe I'm Gonna Leave You" on **Joan Baez**'s first live album, the sensibly titled *In Concert Part One*; she in turn picked it up from the repertoire of another folkie, Janet Smith, who heard the then-thirty-year-old Bredon debut it on Berkeley, California radio station KPFA's *Midnight Special* in 1960.

It is unwise to downplay Baez's influence on the young Jimmy Page. Her eye for melody and ear for topicality was one that instinctively appealed to him, particularly at a time when the British folk scene he might more naturally have gravitated to was still firmly in the thrall of earnest young beardies with their fingers in their ears.

Baez, on the other hand, brought pop to her purity, and that was the breakthrough.

Baez burst onto the American folk scene in 1959 with a momentous performance at the Newport festival, taking the stage as a virtual unknown, and running away with the headlines. Her debut album, recorded in a converted New York hotel basement the following year, repeated the feat without even breaking sweat; her second, twelve months after that, became her label Vanguard's first-ever gold record. All but overnight, Baez swept away every preconception of what the folk revival represented, and rebuilt the whole thing in her own shimmering image.

Her appeal, of course, was unmistakable: a voice of unimaginable purity, a demeanor of haunting melancholy, and the ability to take the most overdone traditional ballad ("All My Trials" on her first album, "Banks of the Ohio" on her second) and convert it into a slice of her own private mythology.

It has subsequently become rather fashionable to downplay these strengths and represent Baez (as Bob Dylan took to doing, following their romantic breakup in 1965) as little more than an empty vessel echoing the most basic elements of the folk revival.

But to give more than a cursory glance toward such elitist snobbery is to overlook all that Baez did bring to the folk process—popularity and romance, to be sure, but also a sequence of subtle rearrangements which were so swiftly enshrined as "definitive" versions that Dylan himself was unable to resist them. His versions of "House of the Rising Sun" and "Lily of the West" both adhere to Baez's prototypes, the first recorded some months before they became acquainted, the second several years after they parted.

Other artists, of course, proved equally slavish. But today, only England's **Fairport Convention** could claim to have had a more profound influence on both the traditional folk and fast-birthing rock scenes than Baez's first two albums, as Page's lifting of "Babe I'm Gonna Leave You" reminds us.

Baez's first recording of the song was credited "traditional, arr[anged] Baez," an industry-standard catchall term that allowed folkies to circumvent the often cloudy authorship of a song by suggesting it was written before copyright came along. Bredon soon came forward to assert her ownership, however, and Baez repaid her by correcting the error in her 1964 publication *The Joan Baez Songbook.*

Presumably Page did not read that book. Or maybe he just didn't read the credits. Because when Zeppelin recorded their own version of the song, the credits returned to "trad., arr. Page," and it would be close to two decades before Bredon became aware of this version of her song. Since 1990, the Zeppelin version has been recredited as a co-composition between Bredon, Page, and Robert Plant.

Copyright problems have often dogged Led Zeppelin. Willie Dixon's music publishers, Arc, had a field day in 1972 combing the band's repertoire for unreported slices of their client's catalog, and they were not alone, as noted above. But even some of Zeppelin's most individual and unique performances have their critics. And their forebears. So we will conclude this first look into Led Zeppelin's roots with the odd tale of one of their innovative songs, and certainly their most influential.

Both in concert and on film, the sight of Jimmy Page taking

violin bow to guitar is quintessential Zeppelin, and archetypal guitar hero. So many others have done it since then, and so many comics have mocked it as well, that it is now almost a cliché, a designation that received its ultimate assertion in *This Is Spinal Tap* (of course), with the replacement of the violin bow with the violin itself.

When Page first took to doing it, however, and for many years into Led Zeppelin's career, it was regarded as a moment on unparalleled brilliance, and a slice of showmanship that ranked alongside Jimi Hendrix's burning, or Pete Townshend's smashing, of an offending ax. The difference was, they drew the applause through destruction. Page drew it with creation.

"Dazed and Confused" was the song that drew the violin bow into the spotlight, a song Page started working on while he was still a member of the Yardbirds. There it went under the title of "I'm So Confused," although it remained a showcase for his abilities, and by the time Led Zeppelin were in the studio to record their debut LP, "I'm So Confused" had become "Dazed and Confused."

And maybe that was when people first started noticing similarities to a song of the same title penned the previous year by American singer-songwriter **Jake Holmes**. Such similarities, in fact, that after years of asking nicely, 2010 saw Holmes finally sue for copyright infringement.

Holmes even knew precisely when Page would have heard his version of the song: on August 25, 1967, when Holmes opened for the Yardbirds at the Village Theater in Greenwich Village, shortly after the song appeared on his *"The Above Ground Sound" of Jake Holmes* album.

In truth, and without resorting to the expert ears of trained musicologists, the similarities between the two songs are considerably less than those that link "Whole Lotta Love," from Zeppelin's second album, to **"You Need Love,"** as recorded by the Small Faces a few years earlier, and which the late Steve Marriott only laughed about when the subject was raised in an early-'80s interview: "We all nicked from each other in those days, only it wasn't called nicking, it was called 'acknowledging an influence.'

Besides, I'm sure we heard it from somebody else. There are only so many fucking chords in the world, after all."

But it also highlights just how firm are the foundations upon which we have erected our opinions of Led Zeppelin's genius. For many people, "Dazed and Confused" is, alongside "Stairway to Heaven" and "Whole Lotta Love," quintessential Led Zeppelin. It doesn't matter to us who wrote what. It is what Led Zeppelin played that really counts.

The Yardbirds, featuring Jeff Beck and Jimmy Page. (Photofest)

3

FIVE LIVE YARDBIRDS AND OTHER STORIES: THE SHAPE OF THINGS TO COME

Throughout the 1970s and 1980s (and, in the absence of any truly viable subsequent successors, through the nineties and noughties too), any discussion of rock's greatest guitarists inevitably peaks with the same four names. There is Jimi Hendrix, the Seattle-born, world-conquering maverick whose showmanship elevated his already stellar musical abilities to truly unparalleled heights. There is **Eric Clapton**, whom history now proclaims to be the greatest white bluesman there has ever been. There is Jeff Beck, the epitome of flash shot through with an absolute restless genius. And of course, there is Jimmy Page.

What do the last three have in common? They were all members of the same band, and not necessarily at different times. Beck joined the Yardbirds the night Clapton quit, but Page joined the group while Beck was still a member; then, after the latter departed and the rest of the group followed within a year or so, he retained the old name for his next group, too. If you like Led Zeppelin, then you automatically like the Yardbirds, because, for a few months at the end of 1968, they *were* the Yardbirds. Or, at least, the New Yardbirds.

The Yardbirds' story begins in 1964, when Clapton, already widely regarded as the best guitarist in west London, was lured away from the part-time rhythm and blues bands with whom he cut his teeth, to replace the outgoing Anthony "Top" Topham in a band whose greatest achievement so far was replacing the Rolling Stones at the Station Hotel in Richmond, just one of the myriad live music pubs that comprised the British capital's underground music scene.

The remainder of the band was already in place: rhythm guitarist Chris Dreja (who knew Clapton from school) and vocalist Keith Relf (who'd attended art school with him), bassist Paul Samwell-Smith, and drummer Jim McCarty were a solid unit of die-hard blues aficionados, while manager Giorgio Gomelsky was a blues-loving Russian émigré who had already discovered the Stones. But the Yardbirds were just one band among many at that time. It would be Clapton who provided the spark that sent the band soaring into the hit parade, Clapton who wrote the first chapters of the Yardbirds' ultimate legend.

SONNY BOY WILLIAMSON: THE SINGER, NOT THE SONG

The newly reconfigured group's first job together found them touring as backing band for visiting American bluesman Sonny Boy Williamson II. As his name suggests, he was the second bluesman to use that name. Born in Glendora, Mississippi, in 1899, Williamson II was christened Aleck "Rice" Miller and might have remained best known as Howlin' Wolf's brother-in-law, had he not taken to touring the Mississippi Delta in the early 1940s and claiming that he—and not the Chicago-based John Lee Williamson (who had been using the same name for years at that point)—was the genuine Sonny Boy.

It was a duplicitous feat to say the least, and one that led to a great deal of future confusion, as songs composed by the original Williamson were routinely attributed to the second, including the all-time classic **"Good Morning Little Schoolgirl."**

Nevertheless, Williamson II flourished. He was a regular on local radio and became an advertising icon for King Biscuit Flour, the face of the company's Sonny Boy brand of white cornmeal. And to prove he wasn't simply a fly-by-night opportunist, he was soon writing original songs at least as memorable as his hapless predecessor's, including his debut 45 (and the future *Tommy* highlight) "Eyesight to the Blind." Indeed, by the late 1950s, Williamson II was established among America's greatest living bluesmen, at least so far as European audiences were concerned.

According to onetime **Savoy Brown** and Fleetwood Mac frontman **Dave Walker**, who recorded his own album-length tribute to Williamson in 2004 (**Mostly Sonny**), "there was a simplicity to Sonny Boy ... the same as Jimmy Reed, it was just a shuffle, but it was a beautiful shuffle. Some of those old guys, you listen to the records and they're out of tune, or you can't understand them. But Sonny Boy's records were so warm, and so exciting."

Sonny Boy Williamson II was one of the stars of the 1963 American Blues Festival, a touring aggregation of visiting bluesmen that filled halls across western Europe and helped further kick-start the British blues obsession; and the Yardbirds were just one of the bands recruited to back him up on tour. But the eponymous live album Gomelsky recorded of the 'Birds with the Boy still sounds astonishing today, even if it did only capture a fraction of their brilliance. Because the Yardbirds were not a musical phenomenon alone—they were also a visual tour de force.

The Yardbirds' onstage specialty was the "Rave Up," an aural assault that saw them raise the tempo of any performance by whipping the audience into a frenzy. Bassist Samwell-Smith would get it started, playing higher and higher up the fretboard, and then encouraging his bandmates to start doing the same. Then, when they had climbed as high as they could go, they would swoop back down to the end, and start all over again. Faster and faster, wilder and wilder, and the audience would be climbing as high as the notes, tearing off their shirts and leaping onto one another's backs. And raving.

The Yardbirds cut their first single in early 1964, after an earlier demo alerted Columbia Records to their prowess. "I Wish You Would," a cover of the **Billy Boy Arnold** staple, did not chart, but it brought the band to national attention, while October's cover of the first Sonny Boy Williamson's "Good Morning Little Schoolgirl" was a Clapton favourite that quickly became a Yardbirds classic as well.

They cut another album, too, the live set *Five Live Yardbirds*, and they rounded out the year with their most prestigious outing yet, opening the Beatles' Christmas concerts at London's Hammersmith Odeon. And it was there, backstage in a theater crammed with screaming kids, the Yardbirds came face to face with their immediate future, a quietly spoken Manchester lad named **Graham Gouldman**, who had written a song he thought they might like.

Destined to become one of the most successful U.K. songwriters of the 1960s, penning a string of hits for **the Hollies**, **Herman's Hermits**, and many more, before cofounding seventies phenomenon 10cc, Gouldman was already a labelmate of the Yardbirds. His own group, the Mockingbirds, were newly signed to Columbia and had intended that their debut single would be "For Your Love," a song Gouldman wrote in the changing room of the men's clothing shop where he worked. Columbia, however, had other ideas. Much to Gouldman's amazement, the label rejected "For Your Love," so his manager suggested they take it elsewhere: "Let's offer it to the Beatles."

Gouldman quickly dismissed that idea, replying, "I think they're doing alright in the songwriting department, actually." Instead, they decided to give the Yardbirds the first shot, and the rest of the tale is history. Samwell-Smith played the tape that same evening, fell in love with the song, and then confirmed his own talents as an arranger by introducing the bongos, harpsichord (from a guesting Brian Auger), and bowed bass that gave the Yardbirds' performance its so-unique flavor.

Gomelsky, too, was bowled over. He abandoned the Otis Redding cover Clapton was determined should be the Yardbirds' next single, and instead presented Columbia with "For Your Love." Weeks later, the Yardbirds were #3 on the U.K. chart, and Eric Clapton was beside himself with rage. Seven days before the single was released, he announced he was leaving the group. No less than anybody else, he knew "For Your Love" was destined to be a monster smash. But hit records were not what he was looking to be a part of. He was a serious bluesman who would play serious blues. He left the Yardbirds to get on with the kid's stuff of chart success, and flounced off to join John Mayall's band, the Bluesbreakers. Later, with Cream, **Blind Faith**, and subsequently as a solo artist, he would rack up more hit singles than many artists could dream of—but at the time he was a purist, and the album he cut with Mayall, *__Blues Breakers with Eric Clapton__*, remains one of the crown jewels of British blues.

The Yardbirds, on the other hand, are the crown jewels of British rock.

Jeff Beck was not the Yardbirds' first choice to replace Clapton. Their eyes were already on Jimmy Page, only for the seventeen-year-old to turn them down. Already one of Britain's most in-demand session men, he had no interest in joining a gigging, working, suffering rock band. But he thanked them for asking, and told them, if they were really stuck, that they could do a lot worse than check out a close friend of his, Geoffrey Arnold Beck.

They did so and, between February 1965, when Beck played his first-ever shows with the Yardbirds, and November 1966, when he grimaced through his last, the group proved to the world that lightning can strike twice. In Eric Clapton, they'd boasted one of the greatest guitar players Britain had ever produced. In Jeff Beck, they discovered another one.

From the very get-go, Beck insisted he was not there simply to replicate his predecessor, even though there were times when it felt as though that was all his new bandmates wanted from him. It took time for them to concede that his very different style of playing, his love of echo and sharp solos and flash, so different from old Slowhand's studied approach, was something they could benefit from. But manager Gomelsky had no doubt and, as the band began building a new, Eric-less repertoire, it was Beck's guitar that dictated his decision-making. Beck's guitar and Graham Gouldman's pen, as he turned up with another surefire smash, **"Heartful of Soul."**

Recording the Yardbirds' first hit, the band was applauded for augmenting their sound with a harpsichord. This time around, they heard space for sitar and tabla, traditional Indian instruments that had never previously entered a western rock band's thinking. In the end, attempts to blend the actual instrumentation with the Yardbirds did not work, a state of affairs that ended when a passing Jimmy Page convinced the sitar player to sell him his instrument for a princely twenty-five pounds. But Beck had the solution. Feeding his guitar through a fuzz box, he replicated the hum of a sitar almost perfectly.

The result was one of the most remarkable sounding records of the year. Only the electrified Dylan of the Byrds' "Mr. Tambourine Man" kept it from topping the chart, but the spirit of "Heartful of Soul" lingered all year long, maybe even all decade, and maybe even longer. Ears that might never have glanced in the direction of subcontinental drones and ragas were suddenly wrapping themselves around the Yardbirds' sound, and wondering how in heaven the band achieved it.

By the end of the summer, the Kinks' Dave Davies and the Beatles' George Harrison were both experimenting with the sitar; by the end of the year, the Rolling Stones were on the chart with their sound, and each and every one of them was opening British pop to even greater experimentation, laying the groundwork for the psychedelic summer to come. And when Led Zeppelin travelled to India in 1971 to attempt recording their fourth album with local musicians, their debt to "Heartful of Soul" wasn't simply evident from the outset—it was present in the denouement, too, as the band finally abandoned the sessions with just two songs (multiple versions of "Friends" and "Four Sticks") in the can.

With a reputation now for every new release sounding startlingly innovative and as fresh as next Saturday, the Yardbirds could have found themselves in an intolerable position. But it did not show. Their next release, and their next hit, was **"Still I'm Sad,"** a Samwell-Smith composition built around multitracked vocals pouring out a mournful chant, over which Relf's vocal positively oozed despair and sadness.

A double A-side matched with the pounding **"Evil Hearted**

You," "Still I'm Sad" notched up another hit, but success was a double-edged sword. As the Yardbirds' love of studio trickery grew greater, so their ability to replicate it onstage fell further and further behind, while the live workload that kept them on the road for more days a year than they were off it ensured there was little time in which to rehearse more than a crude facsimile of the so-lovingly crafted records. The seeds of the band's eventual discorporation were sewn there—and sewn, too, by the financial arrangements so commonplace in those days, whereby the musicians worked their hearts out, but barely scraped by financially.

Manager Gomelsky was the first to go, eased out when the band found a new entrepreneur, Simon Napier-Bell, who offered to win them a decent return for their efforts; according to Beck, his bandmates' greatest ambition was to buy a house each, and Napier-Bell promised they could. He was also able to arrange for the band to cut the debut studio LP that, incredibly, they had yet to make. At a time when the bands who grew up around them—the Stones, the Animals, the Hollies, and so on—were all onto their third or fourth album, the Yardbirds had just two live recordings to their credit. While the charts rocked to the band's latest hit single, the truly sensational **"Shapes of Things,"** work finally began on a full Yardbirds album.

But Beck, like Clapton before him, was tiring of the merry-go-round, and tiring, too, of constantly arguing with his bandmates over their musical direction. His eyes were turning toward a solo career, and manager Napier-Bell—who himself believed the guitarist to be the standout talent in the band—was swift to oblige. Studio time was booked, a song was selected. Now all Beck had to do was find some accompanying musicians.

He surprised nobody. Jimmy Page was hauled out of whichever studio engagement was currently occupying his attention, and so were fellow session veterans John Paul Jones on bass and Nicky Hopkins on piano. And finally, Keith Moon, Beck's all-time favorite drummer, moonlighting from his all-time favorite band, the Who.

"That was a momentous session," Beck recalled. He and Page had sketched out an electrifying revision of Ravel's "Boléro," appropriately retitled **"Beck's Bolero"**; and although it was little more, Beck insisted, than a riff and a rhythm, still it had an energy and effervescence the most crafted pop nugget could only aspire toward. "We didn't have to play it more than twice before the others were onto it," Beck continued. "There was not an ounce of work in it. We didn't deliberate, we just played it through. Everyone in the control room was aghast: 'These guys don't even need to rehearse.'"

The session was dynamite. "Beck's Bolero" was complete in little more time than it takes to play it, continuing to blaze even after Moon, having already unleashed an unscheduled scream of bloodcurdling intensity, demolished his drum mike with a cymbal. The chaos was kept in the recording and then, without even having to think about it, the group slipped into another number, then another. "We did four or five cuts," Beck recalled, "and it just sounded and felt like we shouldn't go anywhere else." So far as Beck was concerned, the only thing the group needed was a singer (he was adamant that "it wasn't going to be me"). But even that was no obstacle. He was determined "we should just get rehearsing and carry this band."

Moon agreed. In fact, it was he who first suggested they didn't even need to form a regular group. They were good enough to become a supergroup.

There were a few things to work out first, of course. Neither Neither Hopkins nor John Paul Jones was willing to abandon his career as a session man, so the search was on for a new bassist and keyboard player. But Jimmy Page was raring to go, and so was Keith Moon. One argument too many with bandmates Roger Daltrey and Pete Townshend made his mind up, and suddenly the new group had a bass player too, as John Entwistle announced that he also had had enough of the Who.

The new band had a name, too. It would be called the Lead Zeppelin, because Moon (or maybe Entwistle—nobody remembers anymore) joked that the whole thing would probably go down like one.

"The Lead Zeppelin," John Entwistle chuckled thirty years later.

"That could have been good. We even told Kit [Who manager Kit Lambert] and Stiggy [agent Robert Stigwood] about it. [Then] we jumped into Keith's car, drove back to London, hunted [Jeff and Jimmy] down wherever they were that night, and told them, 'That's it. We're not going back.'"

Meanwhile, the search was on for a frontman. Steve Winwood, the teenage figurehead of the Spencer Davis Group, was considered, and so was Steve Marriott of the Small Faces. But before either of them could be approached officially, the dream fell apart.

"Moonie needed the Who," Beck explained. "He wasn't about to leave on the pretense that we were going to form a band overnight, and become huge and successful. He just had a terrible five minutes with them, then made amends and went back. Once he found security in the knowledge that he could do this, he probably went back and said, 'Right, I know I'm safe with [us] if all else fails,' but it didn't." And that "took the sails out of the whole thing." The greatest supergroup of the 1960s, a band that would have put even Cream in the shade, had survived less than a week.

Beck remained enthusiastic about "Beck's Bolero," of course. "It's,..very pulsating and exciting," he told *Disc Weekly* in early June 1966. "I'm not going to swear on it, but I think it should go, it's so strong. You've never heard such a thrashing sound." Unfortunately, you were not likely to hear it at all, at least not for now. It would be a full year before the song finally made it out, by which time life for both of the band's key members, Beck and Page, had altered dramatically.

Beck returned to the Yardbirds, but his enthusiasm was exhausted. He was not even present in the studio while much of their album was recorded, hanging around at home instead and waiting for them to call him in to record his solos. Yet it was not the guitarist who quit in frustration at the petty politics tearing the band apart. It was bassist Paul Samwell-Smith, who waited until **Yardbirds** (aka **Roger the Engineer**) was complete, and then left to pursue a career in production. He played one last show with the band at Queen's College, Oxford's May Ball, and announced he was leaving. And Jimmy Page, who was in the audience that night with American singer "Mama" Cass Elliot, astonished everybody—including, possibly, himself—by volunteering to fill the gap until the band could seek out a full-time replacement. The fact that he had never really played bass in the past didn't deter him, and the band weren't going to say no regardless. Page made his Yardbirds debut the following Tuesday at the Marquee.

Roger the Engineer is a stunning album. Caught smack-bang in the midst of their twisted metamorphosis between traditional blues-wailing and newfangled psychedelia, the 'Birds sounded both cohesive and chaotic, completely self-determined and utterly self-composed. *Roger the Engineer* eschewed the hot pop approach of even the band's most recent singles, and instead presented the world with a view of the musicians' own sense of their immediate destiny.

Hence the classically inspired cacophony of "Over Under Sideways Down," hence the freak-out frenzy of "Hot House of Omagarashid," hence the proto–Fleetwood Mac–isms of "The Nazz Are Blue." From start to finish, *Roger the Engineer* was a masterpiece. There was no way they could ever top it—so they didn't even try.

At the end of July 1966, the Yardbirds cut their next single, a slice of deliciously manic psychedelia titled **"Happenings Ten Years Time Ago."** Page played rhythm guitar, John Paul Jones played bass, and Beck simply let rip. It was his last gasp. No matter that he was finally playing in a band with Jimmy Page, a friend he had always wanted to work with—he was still a Yardbird, with all the problems that entailed.

He fell ill, a succession of minor ailments that saw him miss any number of gigs on the band's next American tour, that summer of 1966. There was a swift return to the studio to cut the projected B-side to "Happenings," the kaleidoscopic **"Psycho Daisies,"** and a couple of days spent filming a cameo role in Michelangelo Antonioni's latest movie, ***Blow-Up***, crashing through a blistering **"Stroll On,"** before Beck climaxed all with the merciless demolition of his (hollow-bodied replica) guitar. The best-known footage of the Beck-Page–fired Yardbirds is also one of the most thrilling pieces of rock cinema ever shot.

But another American tour in November was scarred by more absences, arguments, and illness, and in December 1966, he announced he was leaving the band.

Jimmy Page would replace him on lead guitar.

"Beck's Bolero" was finally released the following spring, tucked away on the B-side of Beck's "Hi Ho Silver Lining" solo single. He had a new band now, built around an almost unknown vocalist named Rod Stewart, and bassist Ronnie Wood from another west London band, the Birds. And together they would conspire to create what was, and remains, the greatest British blues album of the age: the utterly monumental and still absolutely spellbinding *Truth*.

Beck himself makes *Truth* sound almost ramshackle. It was recorded, he said, in just "two weeks. But it was a delight. We were so ready to record, because we'd been on the road for eight months, ten months at that point. I think we cut the basics in about four days, then we fiddled around. We added John Paul Jones on bass in a few places, some timpani on 'Old Man River'...I stuck 'Beck's Bolero' on there, to fill it up a little more."

And he recorded "You Shook Me," a song that had been in the Jeff Beck Group's repertoire almost since their inception, a brutal, behemothic barrage of sound that leaves guitar and vocal alike bleeding with exertion, and the very wax of the album melting from the heat. And if you don't believe that description of it, ask Jimmy Page. He liked it so much he practically Xeroxed it for the first Led Zeppelin album.

The last months of the Yardbirds were disappointing, a set of ellipses trailing off one of the most potent statements ever uttered, as though the speaker had simply run out of ideas—or forgotten what he was trying to say in the first place.

Napier-Bell was no longer manager; instead, the Yardbirds were under the aegis of Mickie Most, a pure pop producer whose past hits included smashes by the Animals, **Donovan**, Lulu, and Herman's Hermits—and were, therefore, a million miles from anything the Yardbirds had ever achieved. Most produced Beck too; but even he acknowledged that it was really only the stand-alone hit singles

Beck professed to hate—"Hi Ho Silver Lining, "Love Is Blue," and yet another Graham Gouldman classic, "Tallyman"—that he truly influenced. *Truth* was the band's own work, and maybe if Most had allowed the Yardbirds the same freedom, their time with Page might have passed more happily.

Instead, Most had them psychedelicize nursery rhymes ("Ten Little Indians") or cover Manfred Mann ("Ha Ha Said the Clown"), and more or less record any pop pap he put his mind to. An album, *Little Games*, was recorded, and future Led Zeppelin fans will swear you can hear the germs of the future bleeding through. And maybe you can.

By 1966, 1967, the Yardbirds had developed into an excellent experimental-rock combo, whose greatest drawback was probably an appalling lack of self-belief. Mickie Most, on the other hand, was pure pop personified, his genius marred only by a monumental lack of taste. And when those two attributes collided, we got *Little Games*.

And surprisingly, it really wasn't a bad record, especially if you pass over the regular LP release and pick up any one of the seeming multitude of discs that also delve into the album's creation, via outtakes, off-cuts, and oddities. Things like an oddly playful romp through "Little Games," a smoldering, acoustic prototype of Page's showcase "White Summer," and a masterful reverse tape take of "Tinker Tailor," which simply leeches acid drone and psychedelic comedowns, then blends into the backward drum madness of "De Lane Lea Lee."

The sessions also saw the band return once again to the Graham Gouldman songwriting catalog, this time for "You Stole My Love," one of Gouldman's least appreciated, but most substantial, masterpieces. Sadly, Keith Relf's absence from the studio that day ensured they never got round to adding vocals to any of the thirteen-plus takes they recorded of the song, and when EMI came to add this track to the *Little Games Sessions* compilation album, two separate takes were combined for the finished product. The remainder fascinate the trivia hounds among us, though.

From the same 1966 session, the piano/drum duet "LSD" sadly

fails to live up to the title's promise, suggesting either that the band had had some very mundane experiences with drugs, or that the song really was about money—in earlier, more naive times, *LSD* was the standard abbreviation for "pounds, shillings, and pence." But then you flip the coin and encounter perhaps the most fascinating recording session in Page's entire Yardbirds sojourn, a grueling fourteen-take marathon through "Ten Little Indians," and nobody should be surprised to learn that the development of what was otherwise a preposterous addition to the Yardbirds' repertoire is, in fact, so astonishing.

Several guitar-heavy versions show Jimmy Page in a considerably more favorable light than his Yardbirds recordings normally allow, while other highlights include take ten, where the echo machine is switched on to devastating effect; take eleven, which became the base for the finished version; and takes two and seven, which EMI combined for the *Sessions* album, but which actually sound better in splendid isolation. And the whole experience offers a healthier picture of the latter-day 'Birds than any other release on the market. Whoever would have thought it?

Such treasures, of course, were unheard at the time, and so were any future plans the band may have had. Maddeningly, the Yardbirds barely returned to the studio as 1967 continued on— maddeningly because, almost decade later in a 1976 interview with *Sounds* journalist Mick Houghton, Page eulogized one artist whose work is rarely mentioned in conjunction with his own, but who by the guitarist's own admission was "absolutely brilliant and inspirational."

"Syd Barrett. It was an absolute tragedy that that chap fell apart, because in that nine-month period of the early Pink Floyd all that writing that came out of him was absolutely brilliant and inspirational ...There'd been nothing like it before the first album of the Floyd's. There were so many ideas, so many positive statements. You can really feel genius there. Both he and Hendrix had a futuristic vision in a sense."

He is correct. Across that nine-month period, spring through winter 1967, Barrett led the Pink Floyd through three stellar singles (**"Arnold Layne," "See Emily Play," "Apples and Oranges"**) and an album still routinely referred to as one of the greatest debuts of all time, ***The Piper at the Gates of Dawn***. Any attempt the Yardbirds might have made to bathe in those same phantasmagorical waters would surely have been worth listening to.

Instead, they drifted into obscurity, with a final single, "Goodnight Sweet Josephine," that was utterly unrecognizable as the maverick pioneers who had once made such magnificent records. When the band broke up in early 1968, it didn't even matter that their live show remained an adventure to behold. Hardly anybody went to see them.

Just one relic from this sad farewell could be called essential listening, which makes it all the more infuriating that your best hope of hearing it is on a bootleg, because every time someone tries to release it legitimately (including the band's own label of the time), legal action pushes it back into the hole. Listening to ***Live Yardbirds Featuring Jimmy Page***, recorded live at the Anderson Theater in New York, is akin to sitting in on the guitarist's own future ruminations, hearing him howling through the handful of hits that still clung to the set, the thunder of **"Train Kept A-Rollin',"** the hypnotic drive of **"I'm a Man."** If the occasional note of as yet unrealized self-prophecy (the showboating "I'm So Confused," the acoustic "White Summer" again) is to be taken at face value, he already had his planning under way.

The Yardbirds played what was intended to be their last ever concert on July 8, 1968, at Luton Technical College. Somehow, however, it seemed that news of the group's intended disbandment had not quite filtered into Mickie Most's and co-manager Peter Grant's minds. They were arranging a Scandinavian tour for September, with further dates in Japan, Australia, and the USA awaiting confirmation.

It seemed a hopeless task. Keith Relf and Jim McCarty already had their own future in hand, a new band called **Together** which was not only already under way, but would soon be expanding into the long-running baroque folk of **Renaissance**, with Paul Samwell-Smith called back to produce them.

Page and Chris Dreja, on the other hand, had given little thought to their next move, beyond the vague possibility that they might try to launch a new band of their own. If Grant could get the Scandinavians to agree to a new Yardbirds appearing instead of the old, they were willing to at least fulfill those dates. They began the search for new members.

Their first choice was **Terry Reid**, another of the artists in Mickie Most's stable and, astonishingly, one who simply could not buy a break. Critically, Reid was regarded among the greatest vocalists around, and the two albums he'd cut with Most (*Bang, Bang You're Terry Reid* and *Move Over*) contained some of the most farsighted music, and passionate performing, of the producer's entire career.

His version of "Superlungs," Donovan's craftily camouflaged ode to large breasts, is one of the songwriter's most redoubtable covers—but that was what Reid brought to every song he sang, a soaring voice of almost heartbreaking proportions, an ear for excellent material, and enough nerve to hot-wire a sports car. His version of Dylan's "Highway 61," a live favorite during 1969, is breathtaking in its audacity, despite the battered cassette-quality sound of every surviving recording, and Reid remains one of those rare performers whose failure to break the big time should be the subject of a judicial inquiry.

But he didn't know that in 1968, so Reid turned Page and Dreja down. Like Most, and like most every rock critic in the western world, Reid remained convinced he could make it on his own. The New Yardbirds should look elsewhere, but thanks for asking and, hey, why don't you give this guy a look? This singer named Robert Plant...

And so it was that the distinctly unglamorous surroundings of a Birmingham teacher training college became the setting for one of the most influential meetings in rock history, the night (July 20, 1968) Jimmy Page saw Robert Plant for the first time and declared the guy was such a great singer there had to be something seriously amiss with him as a person. Nobody this great could still be laboring in the obscurity of a band called Hobbstweedle.

Page decided to take a chance, though, and, no sooner had Plant accepted the guitarist's offer than he was pushing forth one of his own friends to make up the numbers: John Bonham, a drummer who'd played in one of Plant's earlier bands, but was now touring the country for forty pounds a night in **Tim Rose**'s group. Again Page had already been turned down by the drummer he really wanted to play with, Procol Harum's B.J. Wilson. So he gave Bonham a call.

It's infuriating to admit it, but American singer-songwriter Rose is generally remembered for just two things, and the pre-Zeppelin employment of John Bonham is one of them. The other is for a song that became ubiquitous on the late-sixties rock scene, the bluesy lament of **"Morning Dew."**

It was Lulu who first brought the song to attention. A Rose fan already, she heard it on his latest album and demanded it become her next single. Jeff Beck heard it there and added it to his live repertoire; and if the Yardbirds had just kept going a while longer, it's the sort of number that would have sounded great in their set, too. In fact, Mickie Most revealed that they did rehearse it, only for Keith Relf to give it the thumbs down, which means it might also have been in the running for the New Yardbirds' own first rehearsals. It was certainly on the menu when Led Zeppelin and Fairport Convention played their legendary Troubadour jam session in September 1970, and it was still around three decades later, when Plant recorded his ***Dreamland*** collection of covers. (Another number from the same jam, Jimi Hendrix's first hit, **"Hey Joe,"** also made it onto that album.)

The first New Yardbirds rehearsals took place in early August 1968, Page, Dreja, Plant and Bonham running through a handful of old Yardbirds-and-others' songs, and it really did sound good. But somehow, Chris Dreja knew it wasn't for him. He'd been in the Yardbirds a long time and had tasted the heights of rock 'n' roll fame. He simply didn't have the energy to start a new band all over again, and with the Scandinavian tour just two months away, that probably wasn't the news his bandmates wanted to hear.

Jimmy Page, however, just laughed and told him not to worry

about it. A year or so earlier, at sessions for a newly discovered singer named **Keith De Groot**, Page had fallen into conversation with John Paul Jones, and the chat turned to the subject of bands. And it was during one of the breaks in recording that Jones turned to Page and made him promise something: if he ever needed a bass player, to give Jones a call.

Page called.

The New Yardbirds were complete, and there wasn't a single "old" Yardbird in sight.

The Yardbirds have never been forgotten, of course, and Jim McCarty still leads a revived version around today, albeit with little assistance from any other former members (Chris Dreja, also a part of the reunion, retired in 2011; Keith Relf passed away in 1976). Anybody seeking a taste of the continuing action, though, and evidence that being a Yardbird might well be a state of mind more than an historical prerogative, is directed toward one disc, the band's 2003 *Birdland* album.

Cynicism initially greeted it, of course. The band had already spent so many years fannying around the live revival circuit that it was easy to forget that the Yardbirds ever were something more than a golden oldies hit machine—that, as recently as their early-'80s semi-reunion as **Box of Frogs**, Messrs. Dreja and McCarty, at least, were still regarded as Legends in Abeyance, capable at any moment of springing a new slice of essential electricity on us all.

Twenty years on from the Frogs, and countless "Oh, dear, not again"-type live hit collections later, the duo's latest incarnation of the Yardbirds released what was touted as their first studio album since 1968's *Little Games*. And, in as much as it *was* a studio album, and it *was* the first in thirty-five years, that's exactly what you got.

But you also found a reunion with Jeff Beck ("My Blind Life"), a lovely psych-flavored tribute to the late Keith Relf ("An Original Man") ... and five more new songs, each one a solid restoration of the blues-wailing values for which the Yardbirds were originally held dear. The current lineup—ex–**Dr. Feelgood** guitarist Gypie Mayo, **Nine Below Zero**'s Alan Glen, and bassist John Idan— was, after all, steeped as firmly in the 'Birds old blues as the

Yardbirds themselves were in the American prototype. And that's the flame they carried aloft, with an energy and—dare we say it?—authenticity that were a delight to experience.

Less forward-looking, of course, were the eight revivals that completed *Birdland*; less forward-looking, but ultimately just as enjoyable. True, the world has probably never really required brand-new rerecordings of "I'm Not Talking," "The Nazz Are Blue," "For Your Love," "Train Kept A-Rollin'," "Shapes of Things," "Over Under Sideways Down," "Mr. You're a Better Man Than I," and "Happenings Ten Years Time Ago." (What, no "Little Games" or "Ha Ha Said the Clown"? What a shame.)

But a vivid taste of the Yardbirds' own importance to rock history was reflected back by the procession of guest guitarists who help out on each—Skunk Baxter, **Joe Satriani**, Brian May, Slash, and **Steve Vai** all got up to play and, although it's safe to say none of the remakes can touch the originals, you will get a kick out of hearing them. "Happenings Ten Years Time Ago," with Steve Lukather and Mayo machine-gunning back and forth, is solidly excellent, and Satriani's "Train Kept A-Rollin'" does, indeed, roll.

So, half an excellent new album, and half a solid rock history lesson. You could ask for more, but you were probably expecting a lot less.

Them, featuring Van Morrison. (Photofest)

4

NO INTRODUCTION NECESSARY:
JIMMY PAGE, SESSION MAN

Long before Led Zeppelin took flight, James Patrick Page was already leaving an indelible mark across the entire range of classic British rock. As a precocious teenager on the London studio scene of the early to mid-1960s, Page played on some of the best-known and most-loved records of the age—major hit singles by the Kinks, the Who, and **the Pretty Things**, cult classics by the Zephyrs, Nico, and Fleur De Lys, rockers by **Them** and **the Primitives**, ballads by P.J. Proby, Tom Jones, and Brenda Lee.

Still in his mid-teens, Page burst onto the London session scene in 1963, adding distinctive guitars to such minor hits as Brian Howard and the Silhouettes' "The Worrying Kind" and Carter-Lewis and the Southerners' "Your Momma's Out of Town." But he also played on one of the biggest hits of the year, **Tony Meehan and Jet Harris**'s British-chart-topping "Diamonds," and word began spreading about this mercurial, yet so modest young axman.

Page was unique among his peers, best friend Jeff Beck included. He had no interest in fame and fortune, or spending his life in a van going to and from gigs. The studio was his natural environment, particularly on those occasions when he was allowed to play what he felt, rather than what a producer or songwriter initially asked for. Because on those occasions, he was usually proved correct.

But if any two sessions cemented Page's reputation as a session-man superstar, it was when transplanted American producer **Shel Talmy** recruited him to help out on a couple of singles he was overseeing in 1964, the Kinks' **"You Really Got Me"** and the

Who's **"I Can't Explain."** Whenever the history of heavy metal is written, those are the songs that stand at year zero. And what was the greatest metal band of them all? Led Zeppelin.

No matter that both the Kinks and the Who had adequate guitarists of their own, in the form of Dave Davies and Pete Townshend, respectively. Talmy knew Page could beef things up even more and rewarded him for his understated performance on the Who's A-side by allowing him to scorch through "Bald Headed Woman" on the B.

Talmy explained his thinking—why he would purposefully dent the cohesion (and, to an extent) ego of an already functioning rock band by bringing in outside musicians to play their parts. It was because he valued the song and the performance more than the fragile egos of the players.

He acknowledged that neither Dave Davies nor Townshend were pushed aside. On the Kinks sessions, "Jimmy played rhythm guitar, because Ray Davies didn't want to sing and play guitar at the same time." And with the Who, it was rhythm again. At the same time, however, "I made a constant decision at the time to have an arm's-length relationship with all my bands, because we were close enough in age that I just couldn't justify hanging around and being one of the boys because somebody had to steer the damned ship.

"So I chose to do that. I'd seen too many bands with young producers who were one of the boys and they were overwhelmed. I was spending my money and I wanted to make sure it was being spent judiciously, so I decided I wasn't going to be one of the boys, it had to be business all the way. Not that I had too much in common with them anyway."

Jimmy Page was a guitarist Talmy never needed to doubt. He knew instinctively that Page would provide whatever a song demanded, and the pair even cut a Jimmy Page solo single in 1965. "She Just Satisfies" lifted the melody Page had already gifted to a track on the first Kinks album, "Revenge," and was the first of three 45s he made with drummer **Bobbie Graham** (the other two, "Skin Deep" and "Teensville," were released under Graham's name). It was not a hit, but it did not need to be. It proved Page was capable of taking the spotlight for himself and not blinking no matter how brightly it shone.

Much of Page's work was done in tandem with **Big Jim Sullivan**, a fellow session guitarist with whom he worked so often that the pair were generally known as Big Jim and Little Jimmy, but he quickly broke out to secure his own admirers.

One of the most influential was Rolling Stones manager Andrew Loog Oldham, as he expanded his musical empire far beyond the Stones themselves. A string of Loog productions during 1964–1965 called Page in both as a guitarist and an arranger, including several delightful eccentric instrumental sets credited to **the Andrew Loog Oldham Orchestra**, and a clutch of 45s by a bewildering array of half-remembered talents: George Bean, Cleo, Jeannie and her Redheads, and so on.

Page became an integral member of the team that powered Oldham discovery Marianne Faithfull to her first flash of sixties stardom, playing on her debut hit single "As Tears Go By"; and when a trip to Los Angeles in 1965 introduced him to singer-songwriter **Jackie DeShannon**, Page brought one of her compositions back to London and handed it to Marianne for her next hit, "Come and Stay with Me."

That same year, as Oldham launched his own record label, Immediate, Page was recruited as the house producer, given a more or less free hand to record whatever talents caught his eye, while being available for any that Oldham passed his way.

Two of the first three Immediate single releases were Page productions: **the Fifth Avenue**'s cover of Pete Seeger's "Bells of Rhymney," as recently revived by the Byrds, and "I'm Not Sayin'," by German chanteuse Nico. Close to two decades later, Nico recalled "a curly-haired boy who was so shy but so accomplished. Nothing he went on to do surprised me because I saw it in him that day when we met." She also remembered standing in the studio to record the song, surrounded by a band that would make the eyes water today: Stone Brian Jones, arranger Art Greenslade, Jimmy Page, and bassist John Paul Jones. (Page also wrote the B-sides for both singles, Fifth Avenue's "Just Like Anyone Would Do" and Nico's "The Last Mile.")

When singer **Gregory Phillips** took on American songwriter Joe South's "Down in the Boondocks," Page was behind the desk, and he oversaw minor hits and monster creations by **the Masterminds** (a cover of Dylan's "She Belongs to Me") and **Fleur De Lys** (Buddy Holly's "Moondreams"), a clutch of heavenly harmonics by the singing duo **Twice as Much**, and the raw R&B roar of **Chris Farlowe**. Indeed, anybody looking for an object lesson in the influences and notions that would shape Page's musical outlook as the decade wore on should certainly investigate the Immediate files, especially those recordings from the first year of Immediate's operation, before Page slipped away to join the Yardbirds.

He is not heard on every release in the label's catalog, and his influence is not always prominent on the recordings he was involved in. But the heartbeat of Britain's mid- to late-1960s pop-rocking soul was laid bare in those grooves, and Page's contributions were as integral to that status as anyone's.

Mickie Most, too, was a fervent admirer, and Page was there or thereabouts on any number of early Most productions, including the **Nashville Teens**' definitive take on bluesman **J.D. Loudermilk**'s **"Tobacco Road."** He unleashed signature riffs across cuts by the First Gear, the Sneakers, and the McKinleys, but proved he could fold himself into the background too, with the steady rhythm he provided for Tom Jones's "It's Not Unusual."

He slashed guitar through a succession of early hits by the Tremeloes and Lulu, and Peter Noone remembers his contributions to the early Herman's Hermits singles as one crucial element in that band's massive success—and also in its breakup, as Noone's bandmates started to resent the session players who supplanted them:

"I don't know how it happened, or when it started becoming a problem. But by the end, Mickie [Most] and I had slowly excluded them from the process, unthinkingly, unwittingly, really with the best intentions. We'd have a session and Lek [guitarist Derek Leckenby] wouldn't even be in the studio because we had Jimmy

Page. Bean [drummer Barry Whitwam] wouldn't be there, because we had Clem Cattini or Andy White. Why? Because Jimmy Page was a better guitarist than Derek Leckenby."

Many of the Most sessions paired Page with another sessioneering legend, fellow Andrew Oldham acolyte John Paul Jones. Born John Baldwin, Jones was renamed (by Oldham) in time for his debut single, an Oldham production titled **"Baja."** Jones then followed Jimmy Page through the ranks of the chart-topping combo led by Jet Harris and Tony Meehan, and like Page (and Jeff Beck), he still speaks admiringly of the supercool Harris—arguably, Britain's first true rock 'n' roll rebel.

Dyed blonde and glowering, a James Dean for a new generation, Harris had everything; his looks, his presence, his attitude, his salmon-pink Fender Precision, *everything* carved Harris out as a role model, and continued to carve him, long after the duo's brand of twanging guitar rock had been pushed aside by the blues and the Beatles. "We all wanted to look like Jet Harris," confessed Jones. Harris himself, though, shrugged the imagery away: "I was a rebel without realizing I was being one. I didn't think, 'Right, I'm gonna have a rebel image.' I just acted as myself."

The pair actually started their public life as members of **Cliff Richard**'s backing band **the Shadows**, but Harris always stood out from his surroundings. Cool beyond words, even when the band relaxed into one of their slow numbers (which they did an awful lot between the hits) or started joking around with a novelty song (ditto), Harris would still be standing just off to one side, part of the band but apart from it too, as though the Shadows were simply the vehicle he'd chosen to drive him toward his main objective—which was to smolder in front of as many people as he could.

It wasn't a pose. Harris was an excellent bassist and, between 1958, when he joined the band in time for Cliff Richard's first nationwide tour (his debut single, **"Move It,"** was still climbing the chart, and the Shads themselves were still called the Drifters), and 1962, when he jumped (and simultaneously was pushed overboard), the Cliff and the Shadows partnership scored more hits in four years than the Beatles managed in their entire career.

But still, when you looked at Jet Harris, you weren't looking at a member of one of the most successful bands in rock history. You were looking at the embodiment of rock 'n' roll as something that was out of control, that had stepped so far beyond the rules and regulations of regular society that even the spotless Cliff and the boy-next-door Hank were somehow tainted by its presence. Just how goody-goody could either of them be, after all, if they were hanging out with someone who looked like Jet?

Years before the Beatles bought their first leather jackets, the Stones grew their first defiant hairstyles, and the Who cut up their first Union Jacks, Jet Harris embodied the face of British rock 'n' roll, as thoroughly as his bandmate Hank Marvin wrapped up its sound.

Maverick producer **Joe Meek** was chasing the Jet Harris look when he designed the singing heart-throb Heinz. So was Bill Wyman, when he started coming on moody as the Stones began gaining popularity. The Beatles' Stuart Sutcliffe had a hint of the Harris about him during his time with the band, and after he departed, George Harrison adopted the same mantle for himself. Once upon a time, the people in pop groups all danced and smiled for the cameras. Jet Harris proved they didn't need to. One of them could simmer until the cows came home. A decade later, aboard Led Zeppelin, John Paul Jones would stand onstage looking like he might never smile again.

It was Jones's stint with Harris and Meehan that recommended him to Decca Records, who hired him as an in-house session man at their West Hampstead studios, and that was when Mickie Most sat up and took notice. Page and Jones have never satisfactorily recalled the first occasion on which they met, simply because they met so often, in sessions for a veritable who's who of British sixties stars. Jones either played on or arranged almost every record Most produced with Herman's Hermits and Lulu, two of the biggest stars in the entrepreneur's arsenal, and he was Lulu's onstage conductor, too.

But perhaps the most crucial component in his burgeoning friendship with Jimmy Page was Donovan, a Scottish singer-songwriter who might have been launched as a surrogate Bob Dylan, with a clutch of meaningful folk songs to match, but who swiftly donned his own coat of musical brilliance.

Five albums cut with Mickie Most, with Jones and Page both present in places, encapsulate the sheer magnificence of Donovan at his peak: *Sunshine Superman*, *Mellow Yellow*, *Hurdy Gurdy Man*, *A Gift from a Flower to a Garden*, and *Barabajagal* (the last also powered by a couple of cuts recorded with the Jeff Beck Group) positively ache with sincerity and longing, but beyond those qualities, they shimmer with a songwriting genius even Donovan admitted was quintessential sixties.

"I realize now that I wrote my best songs in response to events around me, which is why the 1960s were so perfect for me," he said. "There was an entire generation looking for a spiritual path and my music responded to that. It worked like a soundtrack to that search."

Page and Jones, beavering away in the background of Dylan's so simplistic, yet so magically effective songs, were integral to that soundtrack. Hit singles **"Mellow Yellow," "Lalena," "Jennifer Juniper," "Atlantis," "There Is a Mountain,"** and **"Hurdy Gurdy Man"** maintained Donovan as a chart regular on both sides of the Atlantic, while his softly spoken insistence that a better world awaited for everyone who cared for it established him as perhaps the most profound of all the rock philosophers whose worldview shaped the psychedelic explosion.

One song, however, rises above all his others; one song, more than any, speaks loudest of Donovan's genius. It is called **"Season of the Witch,"** and as Donovan describes its writing, you can almost hear Jimmy Page taking notes. For he could as easily be speaking of Led Zeppelin's own alchemy:

"The tune was seminal. The riff is pure feel. My early practice on drums found its way into the groove." Al Kooper and Steven Stills, Courtney Love and **Richard Thompson**—so many artists have flocked to record the song that you could stuff an iPod with the myriad variations and never tire of hearing it. Vanilla Fudge, Terry Reid, Joan Jett...there is a wonderful version by British prog band **Pesky Gee!**, shimmering and spectral, with Kay Garrett staking her claim amongst the most astonishing, and astonishingly unsung, British vocalists of the late 1960s.

But above even those, two other takes are essential listening. The first, by Julie Driscoll with Brian Auger and the Trinity, is perhaps the finest, despite Auger admitting, "I never imagined I would ever be doing a Donovan cover. A lot of those tunes that Julie chose, they were kind of enigmas to me, how to turn them around so they sounded like Julie Driscoll, Brian Auger, and the Trinity! If you listen to the Donovan version, it's much, much faster tempo, and so these things were kind of conundrums, how to arrange them so that they fit into our repertoire, and we give them our own stamp?"

He succeeded with room to spare, and in so doing provided a blueprint for the other essential rendition, as Robert Plant latched onto the song in his early 1990s live show and gave any nearby rolling tape machines a taste of one of the unfulfilled dreams of seventies rock—a full Led Zeppelin version of the song. It could have made even the peaks of "Kashmir" look like a mere plateau.

THE MAN FROM NAZARETH

Not every record assigned to members of Led Zeppelin actually emanates from the Zeppelin camp, although sometimes they are good enough to at least bear repeat inspection. And occasionally, you can see how the confusion arose as well.

Sometime around 1970, Graham Gouldman's manager Harvey Lisburg discovered a new talent named John Paul Jones. *Not* a member of the fastest-rising rock band in the world, laughed Gouldman later, "but a comedian who had the most wonderful rich voice." Of course he was aware that Zeppelin's Jones already had some claim on the name, but Lisburg went ahead with launching his new client's career, and Gouldman marveled, "I still don't know why he used [that name]. It was such a bizarre thing to do! But Harvey always liked the name John Paul Jones."

The new Jones's **"Man from Nazareth"** single was well on its way to being a Christmas 1970 British hit when the original John Paul succeeded in getting a court injunction, forcing the artist to respell his surname *Joans*. The single had already reached #41 on the British chart; in the ensuing chaos, while Rak Records reprinted the label, "Man from Nazareth" dropped from the charts, reappearing in the new year, when it rose to #25. (In the U.S., the name was truncated to simply John.) Its momentum, however, was lost, and Joans never followed it up.

Jones also fell into working with Graham Gouldman, the young songwriter whose "For Your Love" had launched the Yardbirds into chart-topping orbit. Since that time, Gouldman's attempts to get his own bands off the ground had continued to crash against the walls of public indifference, but the Hollies, Herman's Hermits, Cher, the Mindbenders, Wayne Fontana, and many more rode his songwriting skills to glory. The Hermits' Peter Noone recalled: "Graham wrote 'No Milk Today,' 'Listen People,' 'East West,' 'Ooh She's Done It Again'—he was just a phenomenal songsmith. I mean, everything he played to me, I loved. And it's the construction. We turned down Carole King songs and Neil Diamond songs, but we never, ever turned down a Graham Gouldman song, and I, still to this day, say, 'Why didn't I get him in Herman's Hermits?'"

Gouldman's first solo album was a showcase for many of the hits he had written for others; ***The Graham Gouldman Thing*** was largely pieced together by the songwriter and John Paul Jones, with producer Eddie Kramer. "It was a lot of fun," Gouldman recalled. "Eddie, John, and myself, and lots of people dropping in. I remember one night, I was doing 'Pamela Pamela' and Steven Stills walked in. All he said was 'Nice, that's nice,' and then he left again."

While session work continued to devour their time, Page and Jones were also frequently to be found either supervising, or simply dropping by to partake in, the studio jam sessions so many musicians of the age indulged in. The London music scene of the late 1960s was, after all, peopled largely by musicians who hadn't simply worked together, but had frequently grown up together as well, climbing the ladder to musical success side by side.

Such gatherings were never intended to be billed as superstar jams—that was a phrase that came into being in later days, when tapes that had often been lost or forgotten for years, were pulled out and dusted off, then released under a bewildering variety of names. As a consequence, few fans or collectors have given them anything like the respect they deserve, often filing them away as simply a collection of barely formed instrumentals, taped after one too many nights out on the tiles.

Yet a lot of sixties-era musicians laid down some truly dynamic playing when they were simply kicking around with their friends, and the future Zeppelin pilots were no exception. Indeed, some of their most dramatic work, both as musicians and arrangers, can be found percolating across these off-duty, off-guard sessions, together with some of the most fascinating collaborations.

In 1965, shortly before bluesman Sonny Boy Williamson II left his adopted U.K. homeland for the last time (he died in America later that same year), producer Giorgio Gomelsky linked the old man with Page and Brian Auger for the sessions that emerged as the **Don't Send Me No Flowers** album. The fact that these tracks have subsequently turned up across a host of misleadingly annotated budget albums doesn't dismiss their own intrinsic quality.

Neither do Auger's recollections of the sessions. "We hadn't rehearsed or anything before the session. We just arrived there and I said to Sonny Boy, 'Well, what do you feel like playing?' And Sonny Boy said, 'Well, I feel like playing this,' and just ran off a riff. I said, 'Is that it?' and he said, 'Yes,' so we just set the tapes rolling and took it from there. Nobody knew what was going on, but we got the whole album done in three hours, then Sonny Boy was off to the airport."

The same can be said of the jams Page arranged and oversaw during his time as an in-house producer for Immediate, and which lined up impromptu jams by a host of period demigods. Taped in Page's living room while Clapton was visiting one day, then polished up in the studio with sundry session players, a handful of numbers featuring the two guitarists jamming together have, again, been sown across any number of subsequent releases—so many that even die-hard collectors are sick of the sight of them. But Page's liner notes to the original release, within Immediate's much-loved **Blues Anytime** series of anthologies, declare just how important *he* felt these recordings to be:

"As precious little exists of [Clapton's] ability on record between the Yardbirds and the first John Mayall and Eric Clapton albums, I thought it essential to make these tapes available to the serious collector to illustrate the transitional period which helped to build Eric's fantastic reputation."

Page was also instrumental in another precious moment from that period coming to light, an Immediate single release of Clapton and Mayall alone playing **"Telephone Blues"** and **"I'm Your Witchdoctor."** Produced by Jimmy Page, and saved by him as well. Page later recalled that one of the greatest musical challenges he ever faced was to persuade the studio engineer not to shut up shop the moment Clapton started to play.

Deafening, defiantly loud, Clapton's guitar had shoved every needle in the studio into the red, and finally the engineer—a stout-hearted chap who had spent his career working with big bands and orchestras—simply turned off the recorders. The guitar player, he swore, was "unrecordable."

Page took over. Just record the guitar, he told the engineer. He, Page, would take full responsibility if anybody complained. They didn't, and the record still sounds like an earthquake hitting a room full of badly stacked percussive instruments. Which is exactly the effect Page wanted, and exactly the effect he would continue to cherish. A decade later, a *New Musical Express* review of 10cc's *The Original Soundtrack* cast a sympathetic eye over that band's attempt not only to record an unconscionably loud guitar, but also to get it to sound good on vinyl. They failed, and reviewer Charles Shaar Murray sighed, "Jimmy Page's production techniques remain a secret."

Other jam sessions followed, the tapes rolling through some supremely loose, but defiantly disciplined, jams during the late

1960s; and so it came to pass, in late 1968, that Page and Jones found themselves side by side at Olympic Studios, cutting the first album by Keith De Groot, an exciting new singer discovered by producer Reg Tracey. His distinctive vocals, however, were swiftly to be overshadowed by his backing band.

The stars of the show were, initially, the twin guitars of **Albert Lee**—later of **Heads Hands & Feet**, but at the moment content to simply play with anyone who needed some fiery guitar lines—and Page's old cohort Big Jim Sullivan.

Keyboards were the province of Nicky Hopkins, best known at that time for his distinctive contributions to sundry Kinks and Rolling Stones records, but also Page's bandmate in the abortive Lead Zeppelin. Chris Hughes came in on saxophone; the drum slot was filled by Clem Cattini, a former member of Joe Meek's Tornadoes, and another veteran of a thousand sessions; and the bass place went to John Paul Jones.

The atmosphere in the studio was one of barely restrained delight. Watching from the control booth, Tracey and engineer Glyn Johns swiftly realized there was little to be gained from trying to marshal the sessions in any conventional manner. Rather, it was far more productive to simply point the musicians at a song, then let them get on with it. From Willie Dixon's "Lovin' Up a Storm" to Buddy Holly's "Everyday," from Eddie Cochran's "Boll Weevil Song" to Roy Orbison's "Down the Line," the band simply let rip.

Nine songs had been completed when disaster struck. A session was booked, but neither Albert Lee nor Big Jim Sullivan was going to be able to make it. Casting around for replacements, Tracey quickly settled on Jimmy Page, calling him in for the last round of recordings—a total of five songs. Page obliged with some devastating playing, all but reinventing another Buddy Holly classic, "Think It Over," deep-frying **Carl Perkins**'s "Dixie Fried," and blazing across **Lightning Hopkins**'s "Burn Up."

The sessions complete, Tracey had no alternative but to completely reevaluate the results. Though he turned in a fine performance, De Groot himself had been utterly sidelined by the sheer weight of talent arrayed behind him. Indeed, as Tracey listened to the tapes, it swiftly became clear that what had started life as an unknown singer's solo album had instead been transformed into the ultimate rock 'n' roll party album, as performed by some of the ultimate rock 'n' roll party animals.

A deal with the British record label Spark was duly arranged, and the album, beguilingly titled *No Introduction Necessary*, was released in late 1968. Perhaps unsurprisingly, it did little. Although all of the featured players were famous enough on the session circuit, to the average man in the street their names meant nothing. A year or so later, and *No Introduction Necessary* may have been able to take advantage of the Led Zeppelin boom. But by then, it had already been deleted. It would not see the light of day again for close to another two decades.

The birth and immediate success of Led Zeppelin did much to slow down Page and Jones's hitherto insatiable appetites for session work, although they did not distance themselves completely from that world. In 1969, just before Led Zeppelin's own album was even in stores, the entire group was previewed accompanying vast-voiced American crooner P.J. Proby on a couple of songs on his latest album, *Three Week Hero*, while Page alone also recorded with Philamore Lincoln and **Joe Cocker**—that's him playing the distinctive lead lines on **"With a Little Help from My Friends,"** the monster #1 hit whose intro remains one of the most instantly recognizable sounds in rock.

And there was one last, remarkable gasp for Page, and it came in the form of a superstar jam convened by another of the decade's most dynamic figures, **Screaming Lord Sutch**.

Preparing to record his first new record in almost four years, *Lord Sutch & Heavy Friends*, Sutch did indeed recruit some heavy friends—Page was accompanied by John Bonham, for a start, and the album did eventually suffer from the sheer weight of reputation (and, correspondingly, expectation) its cast list accrued. But still it is well worth dwelling upon, simply because Sutch himself remains one of the most magnificent English rockers of the age. Indeed, his death on June 16, 1999, did more than remove another stanchion from the increasingly frail edifice that recalls the fiery freneticism of British beat before the Beatles. It also saved British bookmakers somewhere in the region of $120 million, the amount Sutch stood to win if a long-standing $8 wager on his chances of becoming British prime minister ever came good.

As leader of, first, the National Teenage Party and, later, the Monster Loony Raving Party, David Sutch was better known as a politician than a pop star by his latter years, albeit a somewhat unconventional one. Demanding to know why there was only one Monopolies Commission, Sutch offered policies over the years that included subsidized heated lavatory seats for the aged, lowering the voting age to eighteen, legalized commercial radio, and all-day pub openings. All but one of these have since become realities.

Musically, however, he was equally inventive. Cast initially (and self-confessedly) as little more than an Anglo version of Screamin' Jay Hawkins, Sutch swiftly developed both a repertoire and a reputation that could give *The Exorcist* a run for its scare-your-pants-off shaped money.

In tandem with producer Joe Meek, Sutch was responsible for some of the greatest British rock records of the early 1960, the sound-effects-riven, raucous comic-book horror of **"She's Fallen in Love with a Monster Man,"** **"Til the Following Night,"** and **"Jack the Ripper"** among them; while his band, the Savages, featured such future stars as Ritchie Blackmore, Nicky Hopkins (yes, him again), and Matthew Fisher.

Many of these past sidemen, plus sundry other superstar admirers, would join Page and Bonham on *And Heavy Friends*, and though the album is not so highly recommended as the Lord's earlier 45s, still it catches him in great voice and costume.

Sutch made his first run for British Parliament in summer 1963, and over the next thirty years, his presence graced more than forty elections at both national and local levels. He never won one (although one of his party members was elected a small-town mayor), and toward the end of his life, Sutch's enthusiasm for making a welcome mockery out of the po-faced electoral procedure seemed to be waning, all the more so following the death of his mother, Nancy, in May 1997. A month before his suicide, Sutch announced that due to financial constraints, the Loony Party would be fielding no candidates whatsoever in the European Parliament polls.

It would be the first major British political event in thirty-six years not to be graced by Sutch's outlandish, but often oddly logical ideas, and it suffered accordingly. Voter turnout was the lowest in British history, and in a way, that fulfilled another of Sutch's prophecies. He once described his party as representing all the people who didn't vote, on the premise that if enough people stayed at home, he would win by a landslide. But in the end, unfortunately, simple victory wasn't enough.

Roy Harper. (Photofest)

5

BLOWIN' IN THE WIND:
FOLK AND THE FOLK WHO SING IT

Notwithstanding his background providing sweet acoustic guitars behind Marianne Faithfull's first, folk-flavored insurgence, or the ears he wrapped around Joan Baez and Bob Dylan as he earmarked songs for future reference, few people would ever have described Jimmy Page as a folkie—all the less so after the heavy blues of Led Zeppelin's debut album gave way to the crunchy metal stylings of their sophomore set. No matter how diverse the bulk of *Led Zeppelin II* ultimately was, still the handful of steamrolling riffs that marked out its high-water mark would see the album firmly ring-fenced in the world of heavy metal.

So imagine the shock when the band delivered its third album, and all those musical notions Page kept locked up in his past came screaming back into prominence. Indeed, all four band members have recalled at different times the howls of protest that arose from the ranks of the fan club, once it became apparent that *Led Zeppelin III* was not "Whole Lotta Love Parts II–XIII" but a collection of very different sounds and stylings altogether.

What might well be Led Zeppelin's most overall satisfying album opens with "Immigrant Song," a hissing, howling paean to Robert Plant's fascination with Viking culture, and that sets a stage of sorts for an album that absolutely presupposes what modern critics have taken to styling neo-folk, and placing in the firm grasp of the likes of **Current 93**, **Devendra Banhart**, and **Eliza Carthy**. It is a status, too, that Robert Plant acknowledged when he fessed up to the influence of **the Incredible String Band**, the sometime duo of Robin Williamson and Mike Heron that tormented the mid- to late-1960s folk scene with a succession of increasingly eccentric folk-infused visions under such titles as ***The Hangman's Beautiful Daughter***, ***Wee Tam and the Big Huge***, and ***The 5000 Spirits or the Layers of the Onion***.

See! Even the titles make you want to own them!

Like Led Zeppelin (and, working on the poppier edge of the same thematics, Donovan, as well as Marc Bolan's **Tyrannosaurus Rex**), the Incredibles mined mythology for all it was worth, but did so in a manner that created a mythos of their own. No single spiritual thread or discipline could be extracted from their output; rather, they wove a world that was theirs, drawing in ever more exotic instrumentation and concepts to illustrate the principles their lyricism espoused.

For Led Zeppelin, that process would peak with "Stairway to Heaven," a song whose grasp of mysticism and magic was itself so beautifully wrought that it has now become its own cliché, a cul-de-sac that simply cannot be expanded upon.

The Incredibles, on the other hand, never created an ultimate statement, and so others would continue their work for them; and Led Zeppelin are numbered among those merry acolytes. At the same time, however, the Incredibles are just one of the manifold folk threads Led Zeppelin would pursue across their life span, a process they would themselves acknowledge by introducing their audience to artists whom ... well, let's be honest here. The average punter in Peoria had probably never heard of **Roy Harper** before Led Zeppelin doffed their hats to him on *Led Zeppelin III*; and as we have already looked at the song of almost-that-title, back in chapter one, now is the time to look at the man who titled it.

Roy Harper, at the end of the first decade of the twenty-first century, is a happy man. He is in the process, finally, of remastering and reissuing his entire recorded oeuvre, and rediscovering for himself what his fans have known all along: He has made a helluva lot of excellent albums. So many that it almost seems redundant to look back over his career and play "What if?"

What if it had been he, as opposed to anyone else, who stepped fully formed out of the so-parochial coffee bar– and cellar-based English folk scene of the mid-1960s, to grasp the mantle that Dave Cousins, **Sandy Denny**, and **Al Stewart** ultimately wore to stardom?

What if, having been signed to Pink Floyd's management company, it had been his vision of single-side-long songs that so captured the commercial imagination, rather than those of the Floyd themselves?

What if, having been name-checked on the third Led Zeppelin album, and then having sung lead vocals for Floyd, he had next translated critical awareness into public plaudits?

And what if, at so many different points in time, Roy Harper had shrugged off his role as one of British rock's most idiosyncratic cult heroes and marched into the musical mainstream?

Well, it wouldn't be Roy Harper if it had happened. Would it?

Said Harper: "I've always had a really good cult following, but because of the material itself, because of the depth of it, it's governed itself. It's not really been accessible for the average person who buys records. Something that talks about the nitty-gritty of life in a kind of précised, poetic way, getting volumes of what would be a book onto one piece of vinyl ... who the hell is going to wade through that?"

Point taken. Twenty minutes of "One of Those Days in England," as many again of "The Game," the lachrymose poise of "Another Day," the sad vérité of "Highway Blues"—really, who needs to sit through all that? Well, fans of mid-1980s art-rock collective **This Mortal Coil** did, after a masterful "Another Day" was included on their *It'll End in Tears* LP; and fans of vintage 1973 David Bowie almost did, after he recorded "Highway Blues" with his Astronettes sideline.

An edited "England" is one of the livid highlights of the BBC's ***Old Grey Whistle Test*** DVD series; and, of course, most people own one of Harper's records anyway, as he pops up to sing on Floyd's *Wish You Were Here*, the mega-zillion-selling follow-up to *The Dark Side of the Moon*. And that's *sing*, as in lead vocals all the way through the song, not "sing," as in a few throwaway backing vocals when he passed through the studio one day. Harper may not have many gold records on his wall, but the one he does have probably sits in twenty million homes worldwide.

Born in Manchester in 1941, Roy Harper arrived in London in 1964, aboard the same folky train that attracted Al Stewart, Dave Cousins, Sandy Denny—even Paul Simon was a staple on the scene for a while, and his debut album, *The Paul Simon Songbook*, bristles with poignant reminders of his time in the city.

Harper, by his own admission, was slower out of the traps, but, honed into shape by the months he spent busking around Europe beforehand, the songs that introduced him to the London stage were frequently acerbic, occasionally despairing, and constantly demanding. They certainly did the trick, though. In late 1965, it was an album's worth of these demos that landed him a deal with the Strike label. **Sophisticated Beggar**, Harper's debut album, was released in 1967, only for the label to promptly, and very unexpectedly, go out of business.

He was not on the outside for long. The dust was still settling around the collapse of Strike when CBS had stepped in, sweeping up Harper in much the same spirit of folky awareness as they picked up Al Stewart. But, whereas Stewart would be permitted an extravagantly grandiose entry into the studio environment, Harper perhaps found himself suffering the backlash and being granted a correspondingly minuscule budget. **Come Out Fighting Ghengis Smith** was recorded with producer Shel Talmy, famed of course for his work with the Kinks and the Who, with Jimmy Page on meaty guitar duties, and as far away from the orchestration and strings behind Stewart's album as it was possible to go.

In later years, Harper would bemoan poor *Ghengis*, complaining that it was made way too cheaply and far too quickly. In truth, it was precisely the record he should have made, a set that twisted itself almost violently away from the "folkie" trappings his beginnings built around him, and toward what would, in just a few short years, be described as ... what?

How could anybody, let alone a music critic, have ever created a single term that would do perfect justice to a solo singer-songwriter who frequently worked with a band; to a strumming acoustic troubadour whose best songs lasted longer than very good sex; and to a man who, back before he started making music, got out of the Royal Air Force by feigning madness so completely that some people, listening to his first few albums, believed he hadn't been feigning at all?

Folkjokeopus, in 1968, completed Harper's transition from the bardic surroundings in which he first started, to the more expansive fields of what would subsequently be seen as the prog-rock underground. Managers Blackhill Enterprises were among the architects of the free concerts once staged regularly throughout the summer in London's Hyde Park, and Harper's equally regular presence on the bills exposed him to an audience that wouldn't have walked into a folk club if their own names had been on the door.

Musically, Harper might have sounded worlds apart, but his contemporaries now were the likes of Pink Floyd, the Edgar Broughton Band, and Hawkwind and Co.; and the strange thing is, if you listen without either prejudice or preconception, you can see that seeping around the edges of his records. The fifteen-minute-plus "McGoohan's Blues," which crowned his third album, was only the start. In the studio the following year, recording his first album for EMI's newly launched Harvest label, *Flat Baroque and Berserk*, Keith Emerson and the Nice were numbered among his accompanists.

It is with that album that Harper truly began making his mark: "*Flat Baroque and Berserk* was the first record of mine to go into the charts. For the first time in my recording career, proper care and attention was paid to the presentation of the song. Peter Jenner was assigned by EMI Records to produce the recording. Peter and I got on really well and he was a better overseer of my work than anyone I have been involved with before or since. I had also had a studio upgrade. EMI Studios, Abbey Road, was at that time the most advanced studio in Europe and, over the next ten years, I was to record in near-perfect conditions."

Stormcock, Harper's fifth album, was released in May 1971 and comprised just four songs, which was a dramatic statement at a time when even the likes of Yes and ELP still felt compelled to add a few extra titles to their running orders, to ease the passage into their leviathans. It was a colossal album and, when you cracked the shrink-wrapping and opened the gatefold, a feast for the eyes and mind as well.

The presence of Jimmy Page among the accompanying musicians, meanwhile, reinforced the lineage that "Hats Off" had opened, and Harper himself acknowledged that was the album for which he'll be remembered:

"By the anomaly of the best record of the lot being one of the most arcane. *Stormcock* is right up there with my best. It's been in common parlance for almost forty years now that Roy Harper's best record is *Stormcock*. I don't necessarily think that all the time." But he also acknowledges that, as often as musical mood swings will relegate it to sounding "'olde worlde' ... and irrelevant," others will entrance a whole new generation of listeners ("probably one that had got fed up with silly noises").

Lifemask and **Valentine** followed, two further slices of ruminant majesty, before Harper enjoyed his next public brush with Led Zeppelin, 1975's **HQ** (originally available in the U.S. as *When an Old Cricketer Leaves the Crease*). John Paul Jones joined Floyd's Dave Gilmour in the guest department, while Harper was now fronting Trigger, a band he had formed around guitarist Chris Spedding, bassist Dave Cochran, and former Yes/King Crimson drummer Bill Bruford. Yet, while *HQ* is one of his hardest-hitting albums, it is also—in its original form—one of Harper's most challenging.

"There was a period in the mid-1970s," he explained, when he liked his records to sound as trebly as humanly possible. More so, in fact. *HQ* released marked the highpoint of this mania.

"Definitely! If the top wasn't wound up to eleven, it wasn't good enough. As I've got older, I hanker after a bassier sound, and *HQ* I think, is one of the worst of them all for that. It's one of the best lyrically, and the best dynamically. But sonically ..." His voice trailed off apologetically. Of all Harper's classic albums, *HQ* is the one that should rip your head off, "and it was brilliant to have those guys in the studio, and do that thing."

Unfortunately, he quickly discovered he was not cut out for fronting a band. "Me as Robert Plant doesn't work! When I have a band onstage, I'm not as focused on the audience as I should be; I'm more concerned about the democracy of the band. In order to maintain your quasi leadership of the democracy, you have to give everyone their head, and give every instrument its due in the performance, and I always found myself diluted."

Line him up with the friends who have flocked to play alongside him for his entire career, however, and he has no trouble making his feelings known, or seeing that his wishes are fulfilled. Recording with Jimmy Page, for instance, "sometimes I don't think he wanted to do as much as I'd make him do. I'd say, 'Come on, you can do a bit more,' and he'd say, 'No, I don't see myself on that track, Roy,' and I'd say, 'Yes, I see you on it, Jimmy.'" And Page would smile and get on with it.

Indeed, it's a sign of Harper's towering talent that, even at the height of the superstar-worshipping seventies, critics and listeners alike simply took it for granted that the likes of Page, Dave Gilmour, Bill Bruford, and Chris Spedding (and so many more) should be appearing on his albums; just as they took it for granted that he should appear on theirs. So when 1985 paired him and Page across an entire album together, **Whatever Happened to Jugula?**, it was no surprise the guitarist was just that—the guitarist. The album is Harper's.

1977's **Bullinamingvase** (*One of Those Days in England* in the U.S.) completes the run that saw Harper responsible for some of the finest albums ever heard; his 1980s-and-beyond output is less essential but still enjoyable, and Harper remains, today, one of the most enjoyably thoughtful (or thoughtfully enjoyable) of all the veterans who can remember back to when rock 'n' roll was still young, and a band like Led Zeppelin simply the next step in its evolution, and not a still-unsurpassed benchmark in its history.

"Hats Off to (Roy) Harper," then, was Led Zeppelin's tribute to one of the contemporaries whose vision of folk merged with theirs. The following album's "Battle of Evermore" allowed them to showcase a second.

Led Zeppelin's path had long been crossing, both individually and collectively, with that of Fairport Convention. Dave Pegg, Fairport's long-serving bassist, even played alongside Plant and Bonham in their pre-Zeppelin outfit the Band of Joy in 1967.

The two bands shared the bill at the Bath Festival in 1970, and scant weeks later, with both Led Zeppelin and Fairport Convention in Los Angeles for gigs (Zeppelin headlining the Forum, Fairport the more intimate Troubadour), they played a late-night set together at the smaller folk club, sharing and swapping instruments for a three-hour jam that included gallant stabs at a string of both rock and folk favorites.

Close to a decade later, Fairport were among the opening acts at Zeppelin's massive Knebworth Festival shows in 1979, and so the interaction has continued. Indeed, in 2007, Plant was widely reported to be recording a new album with Judy Dyble, Fairport's original vocalist.

That collaboration never happened (or at least, it hasn't yet). But still the two bands, Fairport and Zeppelin, maintained a musical appreciation society founded upon so many different elements that the one that critics most often acknowledge—that both groups bestrode their chosen genres like no other act before or since—might well be the least significant of them all.

Folk rock comes in many shapes and sizes, but mention Fairport Convention and you conjure up one of the most individual, respected, and long-running groups in the entire history of the genre—the band for whom, in fact, the term might have been coined in the first place. Any number of artists have built their repertoire around folk songs and ballads that stretch back over hundreds of years.

Fairport Convention, however, were the first to bring them fully back to life, electrifying the rhythms and exploding the melodies, bringing music's past into glorious collision with rock 'n' roll's future to ferment a hybrid that sounds as fresh today, some four decades after it was recorded, as it did in 1969, more than three centuries after some of it was written.

Theirs is a long and convoluted saga. Constant lineup changes have seen some forty different musicians file through the band's ranks over the years, including such giants of folk (and beyond) as Sandy Denny, Richard Thompson, Iain Matthews, Ashley Hutchings, and Dave Swarbrick, all of them talents that any other band might have believed irreplaceable. Fairport was bigger than all of them.

Fairport Convention was formed in 1967 by Thompson, Hutchings, Matthews, Dyble, Simon Nicol, and Martin Lamble, and they never perceived themselves as a folk band at first. Thompson explained, "We got into folk not by accident, but not by design either. We all had the same, very cosmopolitan musical backgrounds, and the same kind of taste for everything. So, if someone heard there was a gig going at a folk club, we'd learn a few folk songs and go along saying we were a folk band. Then the next night, there's a gig at the blues club and they'll pay us seven quid, so we'd be a blues band. We schooled ourselves in various traditions, and I think that was one of the things you could do in 1967, which you maybe couldn't get away with today."

Their own earliest equivalent was probably Jefferson Airplane, the similarly constituted West Coast American band who spearheaded the San Francisco psychedelic scene, but sprang from folkier territory than their albums ever let on. Other early Fairport favorites included Joni Mitchell, Bob Dylan, and Richard & Mimi Fariña—solid bastions of the same Americana that Jimmy Page and Robert Plant both adored at that time—and the group's debut album, *Fairport Convention*, reflected that eclecticism.

It scarcely made a ripple, though, and, by 1968, Dyble had departed to join Giles, Giles and Fripp, an embryonic version of King Crimson. She was promptly replaced within Fairport by a twenty-one-year-old veteran of the London folk club circuit, Sandy Denny, and work began on *What We Did on Our Holidays*, the vibrant combination of original and traditional songs (albeit with a nod or two toward Bob Dylan) with which the Fairport story is generally considered to begin.

They remained rootsy, they remained bluesy. But Denny's years on the folk circuit, refining that wonderful voice and those shimmering songs, hit hard on the group, opening their eyes to a new world of musical sources and inspirations. Indeed, no sooner was *Holidays* complete, than the band (now a quintet, following the departure of Matthews) was preparing to record their next album, delving even deeper into the vast repository of folk and traditional songs Denny had brought with her.

Unhalfbricking again acknowledged Dylan's influence on the group's work. It included three of his compositions, including an audacious French-language rendering of "If You Gotta Go, Go Now" that gave Fairport Convention their first and only U.K. hit single, and an epic retelling of "Percy's Song." But it also boasted an unequivocal indication of the band's immediate future, as Denny's wistful "Who Knows Where the Time Goes?" and Thompson's "Genesis Hall" seamlessly wove folk ballad imagery into a modern rock tapestry, a radical electric minstrelsy that was as comfortable in the folk clubs of the era as it was in the psychedelic dungeons of Swinging London. Fairport regularly gigged alongside such underground greats as Pink Floyd and the Crazy World of Arthur Brown, and their examples, too, sank into the band's psyche—a passion for improvisation, a penchant for extended onstage jamming.

It was a spellbinding combination, all the more so for its utter uniqueness. "We were completely out on a limb," admitted Richard Thompson. "There was a very deliberate, intellectual plane that we thrust ourselves out on, because we were a suburban grammar school clique, and because our music was so much further away from what anyone else was doing. For us, what we were doing was the absolute cutting edge, a lot more than being Jethro Tull or the Rolling Stones, or any of the more intellectual manifestations of the sixties and seventies."

Plans to hone that edge even sharper, however, were savagely curtailed when the band was involved in a road accident as they returned to London from a gig in May 1969. Drummer Martin Lamble was killed, his bandmates injured. The band's American debut at the 1969 Newport Folk Festival was canceled, and Fairport came close to shattering on the spot. They would ultimately continue, but there were to be no more half-measures. For some months, the band had wondered what would happen if they recorded an entire album of traditional songs, ruthlessly amplified and rearranged as rock. Suddenly and painfully aware of how swiftly mortality could descend, they resolved to stop talking and actually do it.

It is impossible to overestimate the importance of the album that ultimately emerged from this resolution, December 1969's *Liege and Lief*. With the band back to full strength with the arrival of drummer Dave Mattacks, and with folk violinist Dave Swarbrick also on board (he guested on one song on *Unhalfbricking*), *Liege and Lief* was billed as "the first (literally) British folk rock LP ever" and, for once, the advance hype was correct. Other bands, Fairport included of course, had dabbled in traditional waters in the past. But none had devoted themselves so completely to reinventing the form.

Five of the album's eight songs were traditional, including the epic "Matty Groves," a glorious saga of infidelity, revenge, and slaughter; what was remarkable, however, was the ease with which the band's own compositions slid in alongside them. The vivacious "Come All Ye," which opened the album, could as easily have rung out from a medieval fair as it did from the grooves of a gramophone record; while the plaintive "Crazy Man Michael" stepped straight out of the most ancient traditions of supernatural storytelling. It was a remarkable album on many levels, but most remarkable of all was just how authentic it seemed.

An immediate critical success, *Liege and Lief* effortlessly followed *Unhalfbricking* into the U.K. Top 20, and all but blueprinted the direction British folk rock was to take into the 1970s. Fairport, however, paid a heavy price for their ingenuity.

Richard Thompson reflected: "I always saw our role as being kind of revivalist, resurrectors of a tradition ...bringing a tradition that was defamed and unpopular back into the cultural mainstream." For Ashley Hutchings, however, *Liege and Lief* represented simply the first stage in Fairport's journey into the realm of traditional English song; while Sandy Denny believed it marked the end of a period of experimentation, after which the group needed to concentrate more on original material. Unable to agree, and unwilling to take the middle ground their bandmates preferred, both quit Fairport in early 1970, Hutchings to form the ultimately even-harder rocking **Steeleye Span**, Denny to launch Fotheringay (named, of course, for one of her best-loved Fairport songs).

Again, any other group might have broken up on the spot. Instead, Thompson, Nicol, Mattacks, and Swarbrick simply recruited a new bassist, Robert Plant and John Bonham's old Birmingham buddy Dave Pegg, and headed back into the studio to record the foreboding *Full House*. Then they convulsed again. Thompson departed in early 1971; he, too, launched a solo career, while his erstwhile bandmates simply got on with the band, not only running out a continued stream of excellent albums, but also establishing a national tradition.

The annual Cropredy festival, a yearly gathering of Fairporters past and present, is firmly established among the most important live events on the world folk music circuit. Indeed, there is a gorgeous symmetry to the knowledge that a band that made its name breathing new life into ancient traditions is itself now as great a tradition as any of them—a symmetry and, perhaps, a certain inevitability. After all, as Fairport themselves sing in "Meet on the Ledge": "It all comes round again."

One crucial element of the classic Fairport lineup, however, is lost forever. The death of Sandy Denny in 1978 robbed us of more, much more, than the obituary writers hastened to remind us. She was, as they so rightly pointed out, the greatest singer ever to emerge from the world of British folk rock, the spellbinding voice that drove Fairport Convention to first invent, and then utterly reinvent, traditional music in the late 1960s. But, tracing Denny's career from beginning to end, the full range of her repertoire barely hinted in that particular direction.

From old-fashioned waltzes to modern romances, from wistful ballads to timeless rockers, from gentle blues to grandiose celebrations, Denny's greatest ability was the ease with which she could step into any milieu she chose. She performed in producer Lou Reizner's 1972 stage adaptation of the Who's *Tommy*. With a bunch of friends called, aptly, the Bunch, she recorded an entire album of 1950s rock 'n' roll and, elsewhere, turned her attention to everything from pre-rock standards to modern-day hits. And her contribution to Led Zeppelin's "The Battle of Evermore" has oft been emulated but never surpassed.

As a songwriter, Denny was peerless. Her lyrics are simultaneously darkly intimate and instantly accessible—her words are those of your closest friend, mourning her troubles, celebrating her joys, and spinning lengthy, intricate stories for the sheer delight of the telling. Her four solo albums abound with a spectacular eclecticism, ethereal and earthy in the passing of a breath.

Alexandra ("Sandy") Elene Maclean Denny was already a regular at such legendary London folk clubs as the Scots Hoose, the Troubadour, Bunjies, and Cousins when she joined Fairport, and had already recorded with veterans Alex Campbell and Johnny Silvo, before joining the infant Strawbs in 1967. Their recordings together, unreleased at the time (they later surfaced as the album *All Our Own Work*), included an early version of the song that would become Denny's signature piece, the impossibly moving and implausibly mature (she was just eighteen when she wrote it) **"Who Knows Where the Time Goes?"**

Denny remained with the Strawbs for just six months before departing for what she had determined would be a solo career. In fact, it would be four years before she finally achieved that ambition, as first Fairport and then her own band, Fotheringay, arose to occupy her time. But the four albums she cut with those bands, Fairport's *What We Did on Our Holidays*, *Unhalfbricking*, and *Liege and Lief*, and Fotheringay's one and only *Fotheringay*, confirmed in the public mind all that Denny's peers had long known. She dominated the Best Female Vocalist category in the then-prestigious *Melody Maker* readers poll, winning it outright in both 1969 and 1970.

Fotheringay broke up during the sessions for their second album (since released as the unambitiously titled *Fotheringay 2*), and Denny immediately began working on that long-delayed solo album, 1971's **The North Star Grassman and the Ravens**. With contents ranging from a playful cover of Brenda Lee's "Let's Jump the Broomstick" to the traditional **"Blackwaterside"** (the root of the early Led Zeppelin staple "Black Mountain Side"), the so-evocative title track, and the melancholy "Late November," *North Star Grassman* was single-mindedly designed to raise her free of the folk bracket into which her Fairport years had placed her. It succeeded with room to spare.

Her appearance on "The Battle of Evermore"—her voice a chilling counterpoint to Plant's while at the same time dovetailing exquisitely with his own aural panegyrics—is frequently described as Denny's final, finest hour. But her next two albums, **Sandy** and **Like an Old Fashioned Waltz**, contain their fair share of magical new songs, as did a brief mid-1970s reunion with Fairport.

Denny's final album, 1977's **Rendezvous**, however, was a dark and even premonitory record. Her marriage (to fellow Fairport alum Trevor Lucas) was in trouble, she was drinking heavily, and she had recently begun suffering from blinding headaches and momentary blackouts. *Rendezvous* is undeniably colored by her fears. Rare indeed were the moments of optimism and hope that once underpinned even Denny's darkest songs, and only one song, the fragile "I'm a Dreamer," even hinted at a brighter future.

Sadly, it was not to be. Six months after she played her final concert in London, Denny fell down a flight of stairs at home and suffered a massive brain hemorrhage. She was placed on life support and underwent major brain surgery, but it was too late. There would, as she herself sang on that final album, be no more sad refrains.

Rory Gallagher on a Fender Stratocaster. (Photofest)

6

LOOK WHAT THEY'VE DONE TO MY BLUES, MA:
THE BRITISH BLUES EXPLOSION

There was never any doubt Led Zeppelin were going to be huge.

Manager Peter Grant knew it, when he took them out from under Mickie Most's presumed tutelage and became their manager himself.

Atlantic Records knew it, when they signed the band on the strength of Page's reputation and Grant's enthusiasm alone.

And the rest of the music industry knew it, as Alan Merrill, an American teenybop superstar in Japan, discovered shortly before the release of *Led Zeppelin I.* Recording in London, "my backing band's 'roadie' was a lovely fellow with bushy sideboards named Kenny Pickett," Merrill remembered. "He drove us to the Cabin, a rehearsal studio in Shepherd's Bush where we routined some songs, and all the while he was raving about a new band he was working with called Led Zeppelin. He was telling us how big they were going to be, and when I got back to Tokyo, Led Zeppelin were already rocketing to success. Kenny wasn't kidding when he said they were going to be a huge band. And fast!"

The band **Flied Egg**, who cut a couple of excellent Anglo-styled albums for the Japanese market (***Dr. Siegel's Flied Egg Shooting Machine*** and ***Goodbye Flied Egg***, both 1972), led the way in local adherents to the Zeppelin tenet, with guitarist **Shigeru Narumo** rightly proclaimed the "Jimmy Page of Japan." It was the same story everywhere else around the world, as Led Zeppelin rose to bestride the planet like a colossus.

But there was never any shortage of savage competition to ensure they never rested on their laurels. The Who's John Entwistle recalled how "The Rock"—the frenetic instrumental epic that climaxes that band's 1973 ***Quadrophenia*** opus—was writer Pete Townshend's attempt to remind his audience that Zeppelin were not "the only ones who could do extended twiddly folk-rock jigs." And very successfully he did it, too.

Indeed, the idea that each of the era's undisputed superstars—from Zeppelin, the Who, and the Stones (whose ***Let It Bleed***, ***Sticky Fingers***, and ***Exile on Main St.*** apotheosis effortlessly ranks as the peak of their endeavors) on down—were watching one another's latest move, then pushing to outdo it, is one that could easily explain the sheer dynamism of the era's greatest hard rock. Forever onward, forever upward, forever exceeding your previous best.

But there was a generation rising up behind and around them, too, for whom Zeppelin's sonic and subtle influences were an open invitation to take things to a whole new level.

Blues guitarist **Rory Gallagher** moved to London from his native Ireland in late 1967 with Taste, a band constructed firmly in the three-piece shape of the Experience and Cream. But it was Fleetwood Mac and, in particular, their guitarist Peter Green who gave Taste the confidence to follow their hearts, Gallagher later reflected—a debt he repaid shortly before his death in 1995, when he contributed a couple of tracks to the ***Rattlesnake Guitar*** Green tribute album.

"You cannot overestimate Fleetwood Mac's importance at that time," producer Mike Vernon agreed. "They brought the blues back into focus and rejuvenated the whole scene." Vernon signed the infant Mac to his own Blue Horizon label, and admits it was the band's immediate success that allowed the label to flourish as it did, becoming the primary staging ground for virtually every homegrown blues band of the era.

Fleetwood Mac formed in the spring of 1967, out of the latest convolutions within arch-bluesman John Mayall's fabled Bluesbreakers. Green himself had replaced the Cream-bound Eric Clapton in the lineup, and had powered the Bluesbreakers through the **Hard Road** album, which still ranks amongst Mayall's finest.

Mention the name Peter Green, however, and three phrases come to mind. "Fleetwood Mac," of course. "Genius," because, of all the stars outside the inviolate Beck/Clapton/Hendrix/Page coterie of sixties guitar heroes everyone agrees upon, Green comes closer to gate-crashing entry than anyone else you could name. And "tragedy," because legend and rumor long ago took over from concrete observation when it comes to reporting Peter Green's activities, and neither of them (the legends or the rumors) make attractive reading.

He worked as a gravedigger for a spell, and grew fingernails longer than his fingers. He tried to give all his money away and was institutionalized for his pains. He threatened to shoot his manager, and he was kidnapped by a German acid cult. And, of course, he made a couple of comebacks which were doomed to disaster, simply by virtue of who—what—he was.

That is all in the past today. Green returned to action in the mid-1990s and, since then, has maintained a more or less solid stream of truly sterling blues albums, beginning with the one-two punch of an eponymous live set and a staggering collection of Robert Johnson tunes, sensibly titled **The Robert Johnson Songbook**. Eric Clapton would soon be making a similar gesture, 2004's **Me and Mr. Johnson**, and we are not going to squabble about which one is "best." In terms of purity, passion, and maybe knowing a little about the troubles that can beset even the most successful musician, Green's offering streaks ahead.

He was, he says, "a novice, learning how to approach the blues," when he was first raised to glory with the Bluesbreakers. "But I left John because I wanted to go to Chicago and play with ... not the original blues guys, but the ones who were doing it then. I wanted to go and see if there was any of the old blues feeling still about, and see if I could play with them. I wanted to see how far I could go with the guys in Chicago."

He would make it to Chicago in the end, and the results are preserved across a Fleetwood Mac double album suitably titled

Blues Jam in Chicago. But first Green formed the Mac for no greater purpose than to cut a single for friend and future manager Mike Vernon's fast-expanding Blue Horizon label:

"That's the whole reason Fleetwood Mac came about. Mike was [enlarging] his own label, and I was at a loose end. So I was persuaded, or not persuaded, but: 'Would you like to have a go at it, we'll give you a place on Blue Horizon Records, and it might be fun, you never know.' So I said okay.

"But the thing with Fleetwood Mac was, we weren't really into it. When we started, we weren't really sure we wanted to even form that group. That's why that group was so scruffy and so ragged, such a rag-and-bone-looking outfit, because none of us really knew whether we wanted to do it or not."

They may not have known, so the rest of the world made their mind up for them. Having blown away the attendant crowds at their live debut, at the 1967 National Jazz and Blues festival in Windsor, England, Fleetwood Mac found success quickly. Their first British single, **"I Believe My Time Ain't Long,"** flopped. Their second, **"Black Magic Woman,"** made #37. Their third, **"Need Your Love So Bad,"** went to #31. And their fourth, **"Albatross,"** went all the way to #1. By 1969, Fleetwood Mac was outselling both the Beatles and the Stones in Britain. Their eponymous debut album went Top Five, and stayed on the chart for close to a year; their second, ***Mr. Wonderful***, hit the Top 10; and up there with Cream and the Jimi Hendrix Experience, Peter Green's Fleetwood Mac were the reason the British blues boomed in the late 1960s.

Green acknowledges the accolade, but refuses to accept it. "People called us a blues band, but we weren't. I wasn't Otis Rush or B.B. King. I wasn't a gold nugget like them, I was a piece of nickel, an old antique fork or something. I wouldn't make you eat your food with it because it's old. You wouldn't throw it away or anything, but it's not shiny and practical, it's not gold." And maybe he's right; maybe it isn't. But for a couple of years there, Peter Green was one of the finest alchemists the world has ever known.

Fleetwood Mac left Blue Horizon in 1969, heading first for Andrew Oldham's Immediate label, where "**Man of the World**" went to #2 in April, before moving on to Reprise for their third album, **Then Play On**, the sublime, mystic masterpiece that became Green's farewell to the Mac. Six months and two singles later, he quit the band.

In the light of all that they presaged, and not only because Jimmy Page later cut a truly incendiary version of the first with the Black Crowes, Green's final two singles with Fleetwood Mac have since taken on almost an mythical aura. One, the pensive **"Oh Well"** is a seething slab of brutal self-denigration ("I can't sing, I ain't pretty, and my legs are thin") shot through with Dylanesque disgust ("But don't ask me what I think of you ..."); the other, the sesquipedalian **"The Green Manalishi,"** offers a chilling glimpse into the horrors that now stalked Green's every waking hour. Or so the pop psychologists say. Green has completely different memories of both:

"I was sitting in the back of the car and I suddenly got this most beautiful inspiration of this Spanish guitar I could hear, and I thought, 'That's lovely! Oh, I really hope I don't forget this ...' I was trying really hard to remember it. So I bought a flamenco guitar, a lovely guitar, and I just about kind of managed on it. That was the inspiration for 'Oh Well.'"

The band recorded the song days later, an eight-minute opus that—way too long for a conventional single, even in those post–"Hey Jude" days—was divided in half for its summer 1969 release, the vocal "part one" on the A-side, the instrumental "part two" on the flip. And Green's only real regret is that the world fell in love with the wrong side of the single entirely:

"Part two is the main part to me, is the important section to me. The A-side, part one of 'Oh Well,' is only pecking, it's only the foreword. The good part of it, the part that makes it release-worthy, is part two."

Despite Green's reservations, "Oh Well (Part One)" became Mac's third massive U.K. hit in less than a year. But success for Green was not necessarily the unconditional blessing his bandmates were experiencing, as "The Green Manalishi" made plain.

Destined to become a staple of Judas Priest's repertoire, as well as surviving in Fleetwood Mac's set for years after Green's departure, "The Green Manalishi" remains a terrifying listen, whipped by spectral howls and horror, the true sound of Robert Johnson's crossroads. But Green denies the demons were what most listeners assumed them to be. "People said that song was about acid. It wasn't; it was about money. The green manalishi—money is green, and it was taking me somewhere I didn't want to go."

So he got off the bus and, despite all that has transpired in the decade and a half that elapsed since his return to the performing frontline, he's still not certain he would ever want to reboard it. Because it's not about the money or the fame for him, which is the crucial element nobody understood in 1970. It's about attaining the standards he set for himself when he was still the novice replacing God in John Mayall's Bluesbreakers. "I'm still learning to play like Eric and Jimi, and live up to what people rank me as."

The *Blue Horizon Story* CD box set highlights the sheer eclecticism of the British Blues Boom. The first two years of operation saw the label operating out of a backroom in the Vernon household, releasing limited-edition 45s to a small but die-hard audience. The arrival of Fleetwood Mac in 1967, however, brought the label a distribution deal with the giant CBS, and the floodgates opened: Stan Webb's **Chicken Shack**, Savoy Brown, **T.S. McPhee** and his prototype **Groundhogs**, **Duster Bennett**, the **Aynsley Dunbar Retaliation**. And it was immaterial whether these bands played the purist Chicago-type blues espoused by the Mac, or went the thunderous, improvisational route of Cream and the Experience. At their heart, they still pursued the same goals, reawakening the rock world's interest in the bluesmen who had ignited rock 'n' roll in the first place.

It was precisely that kind of commitment that fired the incipient musical revolution. New bands were emerging in every city, taking their impetus from the blues, and their strength from the sheer sense of unity that bound this extraordinary new movement together.

In Birmingham, the Earth were slowly constructing the doom-laden grind that would emerge in the guise of **Black Sabbath**. From Leicester, **Family**; from Mansfield, Ten Years After; from

County Durham, **Gordon Smith**; in Hertfordshire, **Mott the Hoople**; in London, **Jethro Tull** and Free—all arose with their own power-chord variations on a theme of Willie Dixon, Robert Johnson, **Big Bill Broonzy**, **Leadbelly**. The song, as Zeppelin themselves put it a few years later, remained the same. But the execution was unlike anything else.

Released over a period of less than a year, in what now appears to have been a remarkable flood of single-minded solidarity, debut albums from each of these bands would revel in their roots. Beck and Zeppelin, as we have already seen, both chose the same Willie Dixon number, "You Shook Me," as statements of their hard-rocking intent. Ten Years After opted for the standard **"Spoonful,"** in undisguised homage to Cream's recent prototype; Tull went the same route with their own take on **"Cat's Squirrel."** Black Sabbath targeted more recent developments, covering Blue Horizon star Aynsley Dunbar's **"The Warning"**; and so on.

It was not at these developing grassroots alone, however, that the Blues Boom was making its impact felt. A quick glance at the U.K. charts for 1968 unveils Top 20 hits for some of the most unrepentant bluesmen on the British scene: **Georgie Fame**, **Long John Baldry**, **Manfred Mann**, Joe Cocker, Arthur Brown, and beyond. Archetypal American blues-boogie specialists **Canned Heat** even scored a completely unexpected smash with "On the Road Again."

John Mayall, whose Bluesbreakers were the longest-running of all Britain's blues groups, remembers this period as little more than a blur: "We were gigging nonstop. We couldn't have had more than a few weeks off all year, and that was when we had to go into the studio."

The Bluesbreakers were hot. The past involvement of Eric Clapton and Peter Green had already established the group as something of an academy of blues guitar excellence; now the teenage unknown Mick Taylor was filling those illustrious boots and hauling in as many accolades as either of his predecessors. (No one was surprised, the following year, when Taylor joined the Rolling Stones.)

Already accustomed to extensive blues soloing, the Bluesbreakers saw their vision expand even further in 1968, as they created vast, intricate vistas of improvised musical imagery. Doubtless firing Led Zeppelin's own, imminent assault on the same song, they adapted Willie Dixon's "I Can't Quit You Baby" to ten-plus scintillating minutes—that was one highlight of the band's live set; eleven minutes of Mayall's own **"My Own Fault"** was another. A few years earlier, Mayall remarked, only half in jest, a group's entire set might not have lasted as long as those two combined. Now, they themselves equaled a mere fraction of the entire show.

Extended solos and endless rhythms were de rigueur, then, and aware he was living through a period of creative freedom that might never be repeated, Mayall set about recording his own documentary of the days, the two-volume *Diary of a Band* album, which effortlessly recaptures the sheer energy and excitement, not only of the latest incarnation of the Bluesbreakers, but also of the crowds that came in increasing numbers to witness them.

"We were playing to bigger and bigger crowds, and I wanted to try making a documentary in the same way as a movie," Mayall said. "I wanted it to represent what life on the road was like, what gigs were like, an audio documentary of the entire experience. So I'd take my reel-to-reel to gigs every night and record them. I'd record conversations and anything else that went on, then I put it all together to illustrate the improvisational nature of the group, and the freedom of stretching out on songs. The fidelity of it isn't the best, but for the most part, I thought it captured what it was like to be in the band at that time."

"The" band? *Any* band!

It was through its ability to accept, or at least embrace, such mutations that the British Blues Boom was both born and would survive.

Maybe it was, as sundry subsequent commentators have shrugged, little more than a grassroots reaction to the increasing silliness of the psychedelia which came before it; maybe it was also, as countless detractors have since grumbled, an excuse for numerous lesser talents to try aping the instrumental excesses of a handful of masters. There is a world of difference between a ten-minute solo played by Hendrix or Clapton (or Alvin Lee or Peter Green), and a similar effort by the bar band down the road.

But at its heart, the Blues Boom was the blue touchpaper that ignited every serious musical endeavor of the early 1970s, and the rash of hard-rock bands that took their lead from Sabbath and Zeppelin acknowledged as much when they placed Cream and Hendrix on similar pedestals. Far from all that it eventually came to represent, heavy metal in its purest, earliest, form simply made the same wide-eyed pilgrimage to the crossroads that countless other Robert Johnson disciples have made…and stayed there.

And so back to Rory Gallagher, the man Jimi Hendrix once called the best guitarist in the world. Two studio albums attest to Taste's brilliance, both released in the wake of *Led Zeppelin I* and both learning its lessons; **Taste** and **On the Boards**, two slabs of archetypal blues rock shot through with some astonishing detours. "Some of the tracks," affirmed Gallagher's nephew and archivist, Daniel Gallagher, "could almost be very early metal, with that very deep, almost guttural bass.

"They tried to handle everything—tracks are country, the amazing jazz stuff they did on *On the Boards*—and that took a lot of attention away from that dark, brooding sound. It was brilliant. And if Rory had allowed 'What's Going On' to be released as a single after [they played] the Isle of Wight Festival, when they were really flying, a lot could have changed."

Instead, he broke up the band, forming a new trio for a solo debut album, **Rory Gallagher**, that was as strong as that third Taste LP should have been (had they only hung on to make it). **Deuce** (1971) was defiantly low-fi, no frills, no production—just a hard-hitting roar Daniel sums up as his uncle simply asking, "'How loud can I get this amp and how well can I play through it?' and saying, 'Guys, keep up' to the band."

The masterful **Live in Europe** followed. Unique in that many of its contents never appeared on a studio disc, *Live in Europe* was the first and, in some ways, the best of Gallagher's many solo concert sets. "It's such a good album and he captures the songs so well. Anybody else would have rerecorded the songs in the studio environment to show how great they are, and tried to have hits with them. But Rory realized, no, 'this is exactly how they should sound, I nailed them,' and he never went back to them."

Gallagher's only Top 10 album in the U.K., *Live in Europe* has too many highlights to list. But we must spare a thought for "I Could Have Had Religion," a song Gallagher based around four anonymously written lines he'd found in a book of Irish poetry. He wrote the tune and further words, but still co-credited the song to the ubiquitous "Trad Arr." So when Bob Dylan rang him up one day, wanting to cover the song himself and hoping for further light on its origins, the American folksinger was staggered to discover just how un-trad it really was. His own next album was intended to be an all-folk covers affair, spotlighting his own rearrangement abilities. "I can't do that to this song," the Zim sadly told Gallagher. "Because I can't take it away from you."

Gallagher was at his best. 1973's ***Blueprint*** is arguably the repository for some of his best-known numbers: "Walk on Hot Coals" (immortalized on a classic *Old Grey Whistle Test* performance), "Daughter of the Everglades," "Seventh Son of a Seventh Son"; ***Tattoo*** followed that same year, and then came ***Irish Tour '74***, the subject of both a double live album and a phenomenal concert movie of the same name.

The stars were all aligned. Gallagher was at the peak of his power and his popularity. Readers of the weekly *Melody Maker* had just elected him the number one guitarist in the world, and *Irish Tour* (both incarnations) lives up to all expectations.

In terms of rawness, the vinyl was the way to go; it captured the sound of Gallagher and band as they sounded every night, tight and turbulent, mixed with the magic of a tiny club PA and loud enough to make you sweat in your living room. The movie, shot by Tony Palmer, is a more considered affair; studio fixes and overdubs cleaned things up for what would become one of the best-loved rock flicks of the seventies.

But even here, the polish could not disguise the purity. This is still the blues at their most electrifyingly effortless, and the fact that the two releases shared just six (of nineteen) tracks ensured fans had to grab them both.

The Rolling Stones certainly did. Gallagher was the first name on their list when they were seeking a replacement for Mick Taylor, long before such better-remembered names as Jeff Beck, Wayne Perkins, and the ultimately successful candidate, Ronnie Wood. Four days were spent in Rotterdam rehearsing, before Gallagher hightailed to Japan for his own next tour. They asked him to join the band as well, but he demurred. He liked being his own boss too much. And as for him gifting then with the riff to "Start Me Up"… well, that's the tradition in the Gallagher household, and it wouldn't be the first time Mick and Keef played magpies with other people's music. It took them six years to release it, of course, but it took Rory that long to record "Out on the Western Plain"—a simply devastating Leadbelly rebuild that had been around (in lyrically different form) since the Taste days, and which he now recorded for 1975's *Against the Grain*.

The last truly essential Gallagher album is 1976's *Calling Card*. Indeed, his nephew cites "this and *Irish Tour* [as] where I'd start people if they didn't know Rory. Maybe it's Roger Glover's production, but it's his most mainstream album…you've got the funkiness of 'Do You Read Me,' the great rocking tracks like 'Moonchild,' his voice is really good on 'Calling Card,' the beautiful melody of 'Etched in Blue'…"

Gallagher would continue recording for the rest of his life, touring too and amassing a back catalog which, when remastered and reissued in 2011–2012, comprised a solid seventeen separate releases. And he was as vital on his last album, 1990's *Fresh Evidence*, as he was on his first, as Daniel explained:

"The lyrics on *Fresh Evidence* are that kind of 'Don't give a …'; it's all about having taken so many hits, dealt with so much stuff, the walking wounded … 'Everyone's had their chance, but I'm still here making another record.' … 'Kid Gloves,' with that stuff about being asked to take a dive … It's a very independent record, a very fierce one."

It was also his last. Gallagher died on June 14, 1995, from complications while awaiting a liver transplant. He was forty-six.

While Gallagher blazed, Free roared.

Their dedicated fans still say they could have been as big as Zeppelin, but superlatives always came easily to Free. Across seven (six studio and one live) albums recorded between 1968 and 1973, the London-based blues band formed by Paul Rodgers, Paul Kossoff, Simon Kirke, and Andy Fraser blew past every last rule of hard rock and blues as they pursued their own unique vision to perfection. Across those albums, too, they created some of the most perfect records of their time—the raw and riffing **"All Right Now,"** the echoing sadness of **"Heavy Load,"** the heart-aching majesty of **"Wishing Well."** So many moods, so many emotions, so much to marvel at.

FREE: ALL RIGHT ALWAYS

Rock historians often place Free on a pedestal alongside Cream and Led Zeppelin, the most influential and important British bands of the era. In fact, Free deserves to rise even higher than that. Those other two bands, after all, were formed by sixties rock veterans with years of experience and acclaim already behind them. When Free came together in 1968, the band was the brainchild of four unknown teenagers—a fifteen-year-old bassist (Fraser), a seventeen-year-old guitarist (Kossoff), and a pair of eighteen-year-olds. But they were to revolutionize a musical form older than all of them put together.

When they first met Rodgers, singing in pubs with his band Brown Sugar, Kirke and Kossoff were members of Black Cat Bones, a highly regarded blues band best known for having accompanied legendary blues pianist **Champion Jack Dupree** on his *When You Feel the Feeling* live album earlier in the year. Fraser, the last member to join the new group, also had experience beyond his tender years, having played with John Mayall and Alexis Korner, the founding fathers of the entire British blues scene. In fact, it was Korner who first recommended Fraser check out what Kossoff, Kirke, and Rodgers were doing, and Korner who would give the quartet their name.

The four musicians gelled immediately. They wrote seven songs together the first time they jammed, in April 1968 and, having put Black Cat Bones to bed with a show at the Marquee in mid-June, they were back at the same club three days later, with a new name, a new set, and an entirely new sound—deeply melodic blues, one moment blistering and riff-driven; the next, dark and introspective, led by a voice that could sear your heart, layered by a guitar that stared into your soul. (The remainder of the old group persevered as **Leaf Hound**, an ersatz Black Zeppelin Heep enormity author Mike Edison sums up as having everything they needed to make it huge, "apart from personality, songs, and a decent back line.")

By fall, Free had signed with Island Records and were preparing for the release of their debut album, *Tons of Sobs*. Overseen by Guy Stevens, himself one of the most visionary producers of the age, the album was little more than Free's basic live set, slammed down in a week and ready for stores by November. Listening to it today, to the angular swagger of "I'm a Mover," the warm foreboding of "Walk in My Shadow," the band's youth and innocence still shine through. But so do their energy and the commitment, and the knowledge that this was only the beginning.

Gigging when they weren't writing, jamming when they weren't gigging, much of Free's second album, simply titled *Free*, was already in their live set by the New Year, while a summer tour of America with supergroup Blind Faith saw the band already stockpiling material for the album after that, 1970's *Fire and Water*. Before that, however, the band cut the single that would have ensured their immortality regardless of anything else. That summer of 1970, "All Right Now" was a trans-Atlantic Top Five smash built around one of the most instantly recognizable riffs in rock history, and tied to one of the most universally familiar scenarios— "your average bloke chatting up your average chick," as Paul Rodgers put it. "Timeless."

With "All Right Now," Free became superstars. But, as so many other bands have learned, success was a double-edged sword. In the comparative shadows they had inhabited in the past, Free were free to follow their own instincts, creating the music that appealed to them, as opposed to songs designed to feed an audience. That remained their goal as their fourth album, *Highway*, came together. But, echoing the dilemma that awaited the third Led Zeppelin album in the wake of "Whole Lotta Love," what the group viewed as the next stage in their own development was a far cry from the sounds expected by the armies of fans who'd taken "All Right Now" to their hearts. Free recorded a gently rocking, mellow record that reflected their own musical maturity and tastes (the likes of Bob Dylan and the Band were never far away from the communal tape deck). Their audience wanted to headbang and boogie.

The album and the accompanying single, "The Stealer," both failed, and Free, stunned by the dismissal, simply collapsed. In April 1971, less than a year after "All Right Now," the group returned from a chaotic Japanese tour and announced they were breaking up. One final single, the piano-led sing-along "My Brother Jake," flashed one final defiant finger at the band's hidebound riff-hungry following; the ultra-incendiary *Free Live!* reminded everyone what they had lost.

Free did not remain apart for long. Two new bands formed from the wreckage, Toby and Peace, did little, and 1972 was still a mewling newborn when Free re-formed. A new album, *Free at Last*, followed that summer, but the old balance was crumbling. Andy Fraser quit (he was replaced by Japanese bassist Tetsu Yamauchi), while Paul Kossoff—whose health had always been delicate—was now struggling with a serious drug problem. Sickness and rehab consumed his immediate future, before a drug overdose seven nights into the band's fall 1972 U.K. tour marked the end of his time with them. A new Free album, *Heartbreaker*, featured his playing on just five of its eight tracks, and when Free toured the U.S. in the new year, it was with Osibisa's Wendell Richardson on guitar. Even before they left England, though, the band members knew it was the end of the road.

The group played their final concert on February 17, 1973, at the Hollywood Sportatorium in Florida, returned home and announced their breakup. And, this time, there would be no going back. Tetsu joined the Faces, Paul Rodgers and Simon Kirke formed **Bad Company**, and while Kossoff would bounce back with a new band, Back Street Crawler, his health never recovered. He passed away in March 1976.

Though it was released some three months before Free's farewell, and more than three years before Kossoff's death, the band's final hit single, "Wishing Well," stands as the epitaph for both group and guitarist. Blessed with one of the finest lyrics Paul Rodgers has ever written, "Wishing Well" was the singer's deeply personal lament for his beleaguered friend, its poignancy only heightened by the sheer force of Kossoff's presence on the track, his guitar wailing out its own tribute to the young men he and his bandmates used to be, but could never be again.

If Gallagher was, and remains, every blues aficionado's vision of purity and vision, and Free the epitome of the blues as firestorm of longing and aggression, **Nazareth** (who spent the first half of the decade snapping at *everybody's* heels) were the jokers in the pack.

Not quite the forgotten sons of the seventies hard-rock explosion, neither are they the behemoths of legend they ought to be. On a scale of one to ten, with Zeppelin a ten, and one the band your sister's boyfriend used to rehearse with in the attic in between getting fired from his fast-food gigs, Nazareth probably rank around a seven. They're big enough for everyone to recall a moment of Top 40 glory, but not so big that you could effortlessly wheel off half a dozen of their greatest hits. And certainly not so big that you could pick up a copy of their latest CD (at the time of writing, the snarling ***Big Dogz***) and say, "It's about time they followed up ***The Newz***."

But then you hear *Big Dogz* (or *The Newz* or any of the other Naz albums that have emerged since your favorite), and *all* the old memories come flooding back, from the first time you heard **Dan McCafferty** screech those sandpaper tonsils through a **Manny Charlton** riff; through that mid-seventies moment when ***Hair of***

the Dog sank its teeth into the Top 20; and on to that dark day when, with Nazareth's version of **"This Flight Tonight"** flying stunt planes through your skull, you decided to check out the Joni Mitchell original and overdosed of horror on the spot. My God, who told that woman she could sing?

McCafferty, the voice of the Naz, laughed. "I really like Joni Mitchell as a songwriter. But we did change the song around a lot, didn't we?"

Yep, they did.

The Nazareth story begins in Dunfermline, Scotland, at the tail end of the 1960s, and progressed through the usual apprenticeship of a band with a van: dragging around whichever end of the concert circuit would accept them; linking with one of the labels (Pegasus) that had a finger in the U.K. progressive scene; and emerging, over the course of two albums, as one of the most fiery hard-rock blues bands Britain had ever seen. More than forty years have, we whisper, elapsed since ***Nazareth*** arrived in late 1971, but you would still be gray and toothless before you found a better version of "Morning Dew" than theirs.

A second album, ***Exercises***, came and went in 1972, before the Pegasus label was phased out, to be replaced by the more hits-conscious Mooncrest. **"Broken Down Angel,"** Nazareth's next single, was in fact the new label's first release, and when it drove straight into the U.K. Top 10, it was clear both ventures were onto a good thing. Over the next three years, Nazareth would chalk up six U.K. hits: the follow-up **"Bad Bad Boy"** was succeeded by the aforementioned "This Flight Tonight," **"Shanghai'd in Shanghai," "My White Bicycle,"** and **"Holy Roller,"** the latter edging to #36 in their homeland around the same time a song they didn't even think of releasing as a British 45, **"Love Hurts,"** commenced its rise to #8 in America.

The timing was exquisite. In the U.K., Nazareth rose up alongside the glam-rock movement and, no matter how distant a bunch of hairy hard-rocking Scots (and one Englishman) were from the golden age of tinsel and rhinestones, still the cachet of the era was going to cling to them in the popular memory. McCafferty admitted as much when he recalled the band "shopping at the same places as everybody else, because those were the only places to go," and he audibly recoils from the memory of the spangled tank tops and elephantine flares that haunt Nazareth's most vintage YouTube performances.

America had no time for glam, and no time for any of Britain's other fashionable twists and turns, so while Nazareth's birthplace got hot for punk rock, the band turned their attention to the U.S. and continued on along their own merry path—excoriating blues-rock anthems that defy you to stop your head from banging, your limbs from shifting, and your heart from dancing the Watusi.

"We've always made our own path, doing what we want to do," McCafferty insisted, and it's that ability to keep shining that has established Nazareth as such a major draw on the European concert circuit. No matter how retro it might make you feel, buying tickets for a Nazareth/**Uriah Heep** double bill (the band's 2011 European tour), you could not argue with McCafferty when he said, "People know they're going to have a good time." The fact that the vintage Nazareth catalog has never gone out of print only confirms that knowledge, with the current generation of CDs packing the best sound ever, plus a raft of killer bonus tracks.

And forty years down the line, Nazareth remain a band people are still discovering—and remain one of the increasingly precious few groups of their vintage you'd actually want to spend an evening with, either on CD or onstage. So forget the fact that they never made it to the same heights of hotness as certain other old warhorses we could mention, and celebrate instead the fact that they're still loud 'n' proud.

Paul Rodgers of Bad Company. (Photofest)

7

JUST ANOTHER SWAN SONG:
THE LITTLE LABEL THAT COULD

Vanity labels were all the rage in the 1970s. Ever since the Beatles launched Apple in 1968, and all the more so after the Rolling Stones ignited Rolling Stones Records in 1971, it became a badge of honor for the biggest groups in the world, the most imaginative, and, of course, the most philanthropic, to establish an imprint whereby they could nurture the talents that came to their attention without putting those talents through the grind and ghastliness that attended a contract with a "major label." And the fact that major labels generally wound up pulling the strings in the end (for who else was going to distribute these offshoots?) was generally overlooked in the overall *niceness* of the idea itself.

Apple, of course, proved it took more than open-minded, open-walleted generosity to sustain a functioning own-brand label, and by the time the Stones got their outlet off the ground, the Beatles label was largely releasing the (now solo) Beatles' records alone. Rolling Stones Records would soon follow suit, with a clutch of friends and relations' releases ultimately giving way to the Stones by themselves.

Marc Bolan's T. Rex Wax Co. label sensibly never even bothered looking for other artists to handle. But Deep Purple's Purple Records and Emerson, Lake & Palmer's Manticore, launched a couple of years later, went through the same process of advance and retreat; so did George Harrison's Dark Horse; and so, although we all hoped otherwise, did Led Zeppelin's Swan Song.

But Swan Song still came closer than most to succeeding, its doors remaining open for a remarkable ten years, and its catalog blistering with a select but always solid clutch of artists, handpicked by Zeppelin's members and management, and rewarding that selection with some staggering music. Precious few Beatles, ELP, and Purple fans would ever claim to being a fan of every record released on those bands' labels. Swan Song, on the other hand, was the label Zeppelin fans dreamed of.

The label came into being with the end of Zeppelin's original contract with Atlantic Records, in 1973. Overseen, of course, by manager Peter Grant, Swan Song opened for business on May 10, 1974, and the following month brought its first release, the debut album by Bad Company.

Sixties veterans the Pretty Things followed Bad Company; former **Stone the Crows** vocalist Maggie Bell followed them. Within a year of the label's formation, with Zeppelin's double album *Physical Graffiti* becoming their personal Swan Song debut, the company had four LPs on the *Billboard* Top 200, and those same four acts would remain the label's bread and butter for the next three years. Hopes that Roy Harper might join the label never came to fruition, but 1977 brought the arrival of **Detective**, a supergroup of sorts fronted by former Silverhead (a Purple Records protégé) frontman **Michael Des Barres**, and Welsh rock 'n' roller **Dave Edmunds**.

Sad Cafe and a somewhat anonymous hard-rock band called Wildlife filed onto the label's books in its last few years (together with Page and Plant's first post-Zeppelin endeavors), and maybe they don't quite merit the same attention as the earlier signings. But when we track back to those glorious beginnings, a whole new soundscape emerges.

Bad Company were, Zeppelin aside, far and away Swan Song's most successful signing, and with a pedigree like theirs, that is hardly surprising. Formed in 1973, when guitarist Mick Ralphs quit Mott the Hoople at the peak of their early-1970s success and hooked up with the similarly newly unemployed Paul Rodgers (ex-Free), the band was completed by fellow Freeman drummer Simon Kirke and former King Crimson bassist Boz Burrell, and debuted with what remains one of the crucial hard-rock songs of the age, Ralphs's pounding **"Can't Get Enough."**

"Good Loving Gone Bad" followed it into the singles chart; a self-titled debut album rounded both up with sundry other joys, and seriously, it doesn't matter that the remainder of the band's career was spent not quite touching the same heights of savage brilliance **Bad Company** spooled out so easily. Even in isolation, songs like "Feel Like Makin' Love" (from the sophomore **Straight Shooter**) and "Run with the Pack" (the title track from their third album, in 1976) recapture the sheer blues-rocking magnificence of the debut. No record label could have hoped for a better opening salvo than that, and although three further Bad Company albums (**Burnin' Sky**, **Desolation Angels**, and, recorded in 1982 after a three-year layoff, **Rough Diamonds**) are more or less disposable slabs of rent-a-rock posturing, Bad Company remains a vital insertion into any Zep fan's catalog. And don't forget what Rodgers did next, teaming up with Jimmy Page in the Firm.

Bad Company came to Swan Song with all the promise of a newborn. The Pretty Things, on the other hand, arrived with all the baggage of history already in tow. "Most bands," latter-day manager Mark St. John explained, "most good-to-great bands, have two to three good-to-great albums." The Pretties already had already made four by the time they arrived at Zeppelin's label, and they still had more to come.

The Pretty Things emerged in 1964, hairier and dirtier than any other band on the planet, and a damned sight noisier too. Guitarist Dick Taylor was a founding Rolling Stone; vocalist Phil May was a saturnine beauty who sang Mick Jagger into a hat. Drummer Viv Prince was a lunatic before Keith Moon even thought of combining swimming and driving into a single contact sport. And the two hit singles that broke the Pretties into the great wide open, "Rosalyn" and "Don't Bring Me Down," were so hot that David Bowie covered both on **Pin Ups**.

Two albums in two years, too, set the pace. Both an eponymous debut and **Get the Picture?** served up slobbering slabs of degenerate blues and delinquent Bo Diddley–isms, shot through with the band's own increasingly lyrical prowess. And they were just getting started. By the time of **Emotions**, their third album, the Pretties stood at an unimaginable juncture somewhere between the *Aftermath*-era Stones and the *Sell Out*–period Who, but in an alternate universe where neither band had actually made those albums.

Likewise their best-known set, the conceptual **S.F. Sorrow**. A continuous song cycle, it is superior to any of the albums that are traditionally lumped into the British psychedelic bag (and that includes the Beatles' *Sgt. Pepper* and Pink Floyd's *Piper at the Gates of Dawn*), not only as a listening experience but also as a signpost of things to come. Pete Townshend has frequently conceded that it is the Pretty Things, not the Who, who deserve the accolades for creating the first rock opera, and no matter how badly his own *Tommy* cheapened that tag, he is correct.

Yet the band could not get a break. *S.F. Sorrow* was a flop, and their next album, **Parachute**, followed it into the dumper—and that despite being elected *Rolling Stone* magazine's album of the year, in the years when that was actually an honor to be proud of.

The band went off the rails somewhat after that, sinking more into legend than active service. But Bowie reminded us they were still around, and Swan Song listened. The two LPs that the Pretties cut for Zeppelin's label, **Silk Torpedo** and **Savage Eye**, may be closer to mainstream hard rock than the band would ordinarily have strayed. But they were unmistakably Pretty Things rock regardless, and though the band broke up before the decade was done, subsequent reunions have done nothing to scar their legend, and might even have enhanced it. Not many groups of their vintage, after all, could return with a new disc in 1999 and have the press slaver over it like dogs in a steak house. But that's what happened to **Rage Before Beauty**, and the things are still pretty today. Don't even ask what the best album to buy first might be. You need them all.

The third of Swan Song's crucial signings was Maggie Bell, formerly fronting Stone the Crows—up there with Free as the greatest British blues-rock band of the early 1970s. Solo now, Bell remained (and remains) one of the most extraordinary British vocalists of her generation, with a quality and timbre few performers (of either gender) were able to truly rival, and an ear for rearrangements that could transform the simplest song into a blues-drenched epic.

The best of Bell is littered across a string of original albums, band and solo alike, many of which were hard to find for some time. But recent years have seen most of the key ones restored to the racks, together with a few spectacular extras, a process that begins with the digital rebirth of Stone the Crows.

Stone the Crows' fiery roar remains exhilarating today, with their eponymous debut album's take on **"Fool on the Hill"** ranking among the most excitingly unexpected versions of a Beatles song (and a really bad Beatles song at that!) you'll ever hear. From the same set, seventeen minutes of **"I Saw America"** are equally unforgettable, while the sophomore *Ode to John Law*'s take on Curtis Mayfield's **"Danger Zone"** brings new dimensions to the word *superlative*.

Discs rounding up the band's BBC radio sessions capture the sheer primal rawness of the in-concert experience, while a full Stone the Crows live set, *Live in Montreux 1972*, demonstrated their other great strength. Just five tracks were spread across fifty-four minutes—incendiary versions of **"Friends," "Penicillin Blues," "Love 74,"** "Danger Zone," and some twenty minutes of Dylan's **"Ballad of Hollis Brown,"** featuring the classic Crows lineup of Bell, Colin Allen, Ronnie Leahy, Steve Thompson, and Leslie Harvey (younger brother of rock icon Alex Harvey, who tragically died just weeks after this show was recorded, electrocuted onstage at a show in Swansea).

Stone the Crows split in June 1973, Bell took off solo, and once you've picked up *Queen of the Night* and *Suicide Sal*, the two albums she cut under the aegis of the Led Zeppelin family, a brace of live albums prove the full band's energies were not lost with their demise. Bell's *Live at the Rainbow 1974* and *Live Boston USA 1975* highlight both the old band's material and work from her own career—staggering versions of Free's "Wishing Well" and the Beatles' **"I Saw Her Standing There,"** together with raw takes on **"Penicillin Blues"** and Don Nix's **"Going Down."**

It would be 1981 before Bell resurfaced on Swan Song, at the helm of a new band called **Midnight Flyer**, and if any group can lay claim to the front seat on the should-have-been shuttle it's them, the greatest rock group you've (probably) never heard of. A veritable supergroup formed, at the end of the 1970s, from the past and future ranks of Stone the Crows, Whitesnake, and Foghat, topped off by Bell and producer Mick Ralphs, Midnight Flyer were almost frighteningly powerful, an aspect their eponymous first album captures so well. Bell herself is a revelation, as she struts and strolls, wails, and ultimately steals every song out from under her hard-rocking bandmates. She's a star, and there's no eclipsing her.

None of which, unfortunately, could prevent the band from dying of benign neglect. In the aftermath of Zeppelin drummer John Bonham's death, label head Peter Grant allowed Swan Song to drift into free fall. Midnight Flyer suffered accordingly, drifting helmless for a couple of years before calling it a day. The members went their separate ways, and their union was forgotten. But this superb album (and a mini-album that followed soon after, *Rock 'n' Roll Party*) brings it all crashing back.

Dave Edmunds was another veteran by the time he arrived at Swan Song in 1977. Close to a decade had elapsed since he first came to attention at the helm of **Love Sculpture**, a Welsh rock-blues band who scored a monstrous late-1960s hit with a Mach ten guitar revision of classical composer Khachaturian's **"Sabre Dance."** (Their catalog also includes another version of the ubiquitous "Morning Dew.")

Love Sculpture broke up at the dawn of the 1970s, and Edmunds went solo, promptly scoring a U.K. chart topper (and an American #4) with a gloriously ramshackle version of Smiley Lewis's **"I Hear You Knocking."** But record-company shenanigans ensured two years would elapse before the accompanying *Rockpile* album emerged, and Edmunds spent much of the next two years working on, and at, Rockfield Studios in Monmouth, Wales, a cozy setup where he wasn't simply producer-in-residence, but also had the time and wherewithal to fashion one of the most exciting musical hybrids of the age, a rock 'n' roll revivalist sound that (with a sideways glance at the simultaneous glam phenomenon) reimagined Phil Spector in the twenty-first century.

Solo hits **"Baby I Love You"** and the exquisite **"Born to Be with You,"** the album *Subtle as a Flying Mallet*, and his contributions to the soundtrack of the movie *Stardust* (in which he also costarred with David Essex and Larry Hagman), confirmed Edmunds's understated genius, at the same time as he seemingly deliberately kept a full-fledged commercial breakthrough at arm's length. But it was the formation of Rockpile, with songwriter Nick Lowe, in 1976, that would lead him into his period of greatest success, even if the band seemed likewise bound to remain utterly obscure. How many other groups are formed around the knowledge that the members' individual record contracts would prohibit them from actually recording under their own names?

Nick Lowe's *Labour of Lust* and Edmunds's Swan Song debut, *Repeat When Necessary*, were both Rockpile concoctions; and so was **"I Knew the Bride,"** a positively irresistible blaze of rock 'n' rolling revivalism that brought Edmunds (and Swan Song) a major 1977 hit. Further hits **"Girls Talk"** (written by Elvis Costello), **"Crawling from the Wreckage"** (by Graham Parker), **"Queen of Hearts"** (Hank DeVito), and **"Singing the Blues"** (a mid-1950s hit for English proto-rocker Tommy Steele) followed, and how ironic it was that by the time Rockpile were finally permitted to record together under their own name, 1980's *Seconds of Pleasure* LP, the group was itself just moments from death.

They broke up soon after the album's release, but the spirit of Rockpile would live on, both in Edmunds's continued career and in Robert Plant's. What, after all, were **the Honeydrippers** but a reminder of just how remarkably the past could be updated to sound like it was still happening today, a sonic alchemy Rockpile made reality every time they played?

Eddie Cochran, circa late 1950s. (Photofest)

8

C'MON EVERYBODY:
COVERING THE CLASSICS

Deep within the dark and muddy waters of Led Zeppelin's bootleg discography—that is, for those who remain ignorant of such things, the wealth of unauthorized live and outtake recordings that sundry evildoers once pressed up of their own accord, to sell to fans who could not get enough of the real thing—there exists a nine-song tape of a Led Zeppelin soundcheck, dating from Chicago, July 6, 1973.

The sound quality is stellar, which is not always the case with Zeppelin's (or anyone else's) bootlegs, and the performance is dynamite. Listening to a tape of the rest of the night, in fact, you could almost say the audience was cheated. It was the concert that was the soundcheck, because the soundcheck was everything Led Zeppelin should be: inspired, incisive, and totally, ruthlessly in your face.

And they did it without playing a single song their album-owning public would have recognized from their own canon.

1973–1974 was an odd time in rock. In the U.K., glam rock was the order of the day, a spangly, glittery creation that pondered one of the oddest equations modern rock has ever had to grapple with: What would have happened if 1950s rock 'n' roll had been created exclusively by bisexual spacemen? And we're not just talking about David Bowie here. Marc Bolan, Elton John, Gary Glitter, **the Sweet**, Mud, even early **Queen**—all drove into the consciousness of the early to mid-1970s from that same point of querulous absurdity, all donned silver and face paint and enough rhinestones to dam a German river, and then rewired old Chuck Berry through a teenage magazine's problem page.

"Dear Doctor: My best friend told me that Robert Plant's nickname is 'Percy,' which is also a slang word for *penis*. I have a poster of him on my bedroom wall, and his trousers are very, very tight. What does this mean?"

"Dear Worried from Wyoming: It means…"

In late 1973, both Bowie and Roxy Music frontman Bryan Ferry set about recording albums comprised exclusively of covers of the music that had soundtracked their childhoods. So—a musical generation ahead them, but still firing on all rocking cylinders—did John Lennon, and the songs they picked on were instructive enough. Bowie's *Pin Ups* grabbed two Yardbirds oldies (the Clapton-era "I Wish You Would" and the Beck-bouncing showcase "Shapes of Things"), the first two Pretty Things hits, and the Who's "I Can't Explain" and "Anyway Anyhow Anywhere," plus a clutch of other sixties mod rockers which, if Jimmy Page didn't play on the original versions, he could have.

Ferry's *These Foolish Things* dug deeper, preferring pre-rock standards to anything modern, but still putting Dylan and the Stones through the magical mincer; and Lennon sank smack in between, with an album he called *Rock 'n' Roll* because that was the era he was going for.

Zeppelin's Chicago soundcheck is the fourth album in that sequence because, like Bowie, Ferry, and Lennon, they left their audience's expectations behind and played wholly for themselves. It was neither the first, nor the only, occasion upon which the band warmed up with a handful of golden oldies; indeed, entire albums' worth of Zeppelinized covers can be drawn from across their concert catalog—particularly in the early days, before the live show became so ruthlessly choreographed that neither hell nor high water could disrupt the set list.

But Chicago is a brilliant snapshot all the same, because it focuses on three influences the band members have rarely, if ever, taken time to talk about, but whose music plays in their heads like a radio regardless, shaping the thoughts that dance under their thinking.

We will call it *Zeppelin Unclothed.*

Chuck Berry takes the lion's share of the writing credits, and that is how it should be. Perhaps more than any other of the classic rockers who emerged from the late-1950s American rock 'n' roll scene (and that includes Elvis, **Gene Vincent**, and Buddy Holly), Berry was the quintessential figure, one whose background, output, and even record label (Chicago's Chess Records) hopscotched between the blues of the past and the rock of the future. Certainly his songbook can lay claim to being among the most frequently visited of any writer; from **"Johnny B. Goode"** to **"Bye Bye Johnny,"** from **"Carol"** to **"Maybellene,"** Berry wrote the songs the British Invasion was built upon, with even the super-songwriting Lennon and McCartney unable to resist his "Roll Over Beethoven." The rest of the musical universe simply followed in their footsteps.

Led Zeppelin were no less immune to Berry's charms. Hark to the strains of **"Nadine"** and **"School Days," "Reelin' and Rockin',"** and **"Round and Round"** (a song that Bowie, too, took a fancy to, and which almost made it onto his *The Rise and Fall of Ziggy Stardust and the Spiders from Mars* concept breakthrough), and the sheer simplicity of Berry's music and lyrics is something Led Zeppelin never lost sight of, no matter how contrarily complicated their own music may have become.

The fact is—and it's as true today, forty years on, as it was in 1973, when less than two decades had elapsed since Berry's prime—laying your hands on a good Chuck Berry compilation album is like treating your ears to the entire history of rock 'n' roll, all condensed into one single sitting. It's why a lot of his old fans don't need anything else. Chuck said it all.

Or almost all. A little short of midway through the tape, and Page peels out a guitar introduction that feels familiar even if you've never heard the song. **"Shakin' All Over"** was the first and only U.K. #1 for **Johnny Kidd and the Pirates**, at the very end of the original rock 'n' roll era, in summer 1960. Some people have even described it as the first true British rock 'n' roll song—which isn't true at all, because the real originator is also on this tape.

But it isn't hard to see why people make that mistake. Plant sings the song as naturally as breathing, and Pirates guitarist Mick Green recalled all four Zeppelin members being regulars at the band's live performances, both in the 1960s and thereafter, when the group reunited a decade after frontman Kidd's death in a mid-1960s road accident. "Shakin' All Over," meanwhile, remains a key component in Led Zeppelin's soul.

There it is joined by Cliff Richard and the Shadows, chronologically and creatively the first British rock 'n' roll band to answer the Americans' clarion call, with a run of hit singles that kicked off with "Move It" in 1958, and—for singer Richard at least—is still under way, more than half a century later.

"Move It" (his first hit), **"Dynamite"** (the B-side of his sixth), and **"Please Don't Tease"** (his ninth) are the songs that kick off the soundcheck, and again, the band are not simply playing oldies. They are playing their own DNA, because any British artist who was appreciating music in the late 1950s and pre-Beatles sixties, and who claims not to have been influenced by Cliff and the Shadows, is either a liar or a jazzman.

CLIFF RICHARD: HE MOVED IT

C liff has been compilationed to death over the decades; attempting to even calculate the number of separate CDs his early hits appear on is like counting the gray hairs in an old man's beard. There is one package, however, that stands as essential listening for anybody wanting to step into the early teenage Cliff's shoes, to discover the music that first fired his rocking genes.

In the starkest terms, Cliff Richard's career can be broken down into two periods of undeniable dynamism (1958–66 and 1975–81), one of absolute foundering (1967–74) and one (1981–present) during which he became so much a part of the furniture that neither critical nor commercial criteria even apply. *The Rock 'n' Roll Years 1958–1963*, as its title suggests, concentrates on the first of these eras—four discs of hits, rarities, obscurities, and the utterly unknown that run in strict chronology through Richard's first eight albums, twenty-plus EPs, and twenty-three singles, to allow his career to unfold as the fans would have heard it, back in the day. (Although the gaps between singles and albums are shorter.) And it's not Cliff's own story, either. *The Rock 'n' Roll Years* is also a macrocosmic examination of his backing band, the Shadows—from whose lineup sprang Page and Jones's old employers Jet Harris and Tony Meehan, and from whose example erupted nigh on to every British guitar hero of the age.

For, while it was Cliff who fronted the records and sang the songs, the story of this remarkable act—and the even more remarkable impact it had on the musical tastes of an entire generation—really begins with a man named Hank.

Brian "Hank Marvin" Rankin was not the first rock 'n' roll guitar-slinger, of course. He wasn't even the first British one. But he was the first who not only looked good and sounded better, but also made it all seem so easy. Still in his teens, the bespectacled youth was nobody's idea of a teenage idol—even without the glasses (which at least gave him a hint of the Buddy Holly); he was tall enough to seem gawky, and gawky enough to look goofy. But put a guitar in his hand and a band at his back, and he was a god, which really wasn't something you expected anybody to say about a British rock 'n' roller in the late 1950s.

Rock 'n' roll was American; its heroes, naturally, were Americans as well, exotic invaders who filled teenage ears with drawling accents and an erotic twang, a world of lurid neon, fin-backed Chevys, and chick-infested soda pops a million miles from the drab gray of Anytown, England. Then Cliff and Hank and the Shadows came along, and suddenly rock 'n' roll was global, and its possibilities universal. And in villages, towns, and cities the length and breadth of the land, kids were switching on their weekly dose of televised *Oh Boy* and realizing: *If they can do it, so can I!*

They could, as well. **Pink Fairies** guitarist Larry Wallis spoke for an entire generation when he recalled, "When I heard Hank B. Marvin on the [first] *Cliff Richard* album, and saw the pic of him with a Vox solid-body guitar, all was truly lost." **Whitesnake's** Mick Moody affectionately remembers the secondhand guitar his father bought him, on which he learned to play the Shadows' "Apache" on one string; Ritchie Blackmore, Jeff Beck, Jimmy Page, and John Lennon were all Hank nuts, and songwriter Graham Gouldman remembers learning the bass guitar by playing his Shadows 45s at 33 rpm.

Whether clowning behind Cliff, or stepping out in their own right (they scored their first instrumental hit, **"Apache,"** in 1960), the Shadows—with Marvin's guitar fully to the fore—dominated British rock in the years before the Beatles. Between the success of "Move It" in late 1958 and the Fab's first chart-topper in early 1963, the team racked up more than thirty U.K. hits, and no fewer than ten of them topped the chart. Which meant that even if an aspiring young musician didn't especially care for the band, still there was no escape from them.

Marvin wasn't the only icon in the Shadows, of course. Rhythm guitarist Bruce Welch attracted the axmen who didn't want to have all the limelight. Drummers looked to Tony Meehan, and we have already seen how bassists looked to Jet Harris...in fact, *everybody* looked at Jet Harris, even when they knew they ought to be concentrating on Marvin's winged fingertips. Cliff was simply the scrumptious icing on an already delicious cake.

With Cliff Richard's blueprint firmly in hand, the session-man beginnings of Jimmy Page and John Paul Jones helped create much of the music that ultimately fed into Led Zeppelin's own private jukebox. But it was Robert Plant who acted as its curator, both throughout Led Zeppelin's own life span, as he ad-libbed whatever great oldie came to mind in the midst of a group jam, and in the decades after the band's dissolution.

Plant's solo career, while no more prone than Zeppelin's to delve into the worlds of other writers, has nevertheless kept a number of musical flames burning, a process that climaxed first with his creation of the on/off side project the Honeydrippers in 1981; then with 2002's shimmering *Dreamland*; and finally, with his 2007–

2008 union with singer Alison Krauss, to record the so-sensational *Raising Sand* collection of blisteringly lackadaisical Americana.

Tom Waits, Gene Clark, the Everly Brothers, and more filed through the duo's surprisingly harmonic harmonizing to create one of the few truly deserving Grammy Album of the Year award winners of recent memory—which in turn earns an impatient shrug from anyone who has followed Plant's career this long because, really, he's been playing with gritty bluegrassed blues for years, so how come it was only being remarked upon now?

Still, the timing was interesting. The year before *Raising Sand* had seen Plant's entire post-Zeppelin output memorialized by **Nine Lives**, an all-encompassing box set many people regarded as the final word on his solo career. Well, that's how it normally works. It would be grotesquely insincere to describe every box set as a gravestone at the head of an artist's artistry, as **Neil Young** and Bob Dylan would both hasten to demonstrate. But still, more boxes serve as the end of a sentence than the comma that pauses halfway, all the more so when they devour a span as great as *Nine Lives* took on.

At the time of the box set's release, no less than twenty-seven years had elapsed since Robert Plant last sang with Led Zeppelin ... a lifetime for the likes of Brian Jones, Jimi Hendrix, and Kurt Cobain; a long time for everybody else. And it must be said, while his erstwhile bandmates had seldom truly escaped the shadow of their behemothic past, Plant had scarcely ever looked back.

Oh, there have been lapses—the *Unledded* reunion, for one, Live Aid for another. But, from the moment Plant's **Pictures at Eleven** debut album let it be known that the pomp and circumstance of classic Zep was a thing of the past, nothing—not even that so distinctive voice, draped around the trampled undergrowth of the album's opening, "Burning Down One Side"—was going to send him hastening back to old pastures. Indeed, forget the cultural impact Zeppelin made, and allow their output to stand wholly on its own musical merits, and great swaths of Plant's solo output dwarf the band's own accomplishments, all the more so since the singer himself was free to develop at a rate Zeppelin could never have permitted.

Light years divide **The Principle of Moments**, his second album, from **Shaken 'n' Stirred**, his fourth, a gulf that was only amplified by the sheer joy of *The Honeydrippers Volume One*, the six-track mini-album that landed in-between times, and catapulted Plant once again back to a clutch of formative influences.

Roy Brown's "Rockin' at Midnight" was the late-1940s stomper that succeeded his earlier "Good Rockin' Tonight" on the chart, but precedes it on the Honeydrippers album; "I Got a Woman" was a characteristically raucous Ray Charles raver; "Young Boy Blues" was a **Doc Pomus**/Phil Spector number that titled Ben E. King's fourth album; and "Sea of Love" was a U.S. hit for Phil Phillips that Plant would have first heard in the hands of **Marty Wilde**, another of Britain's first-wave rock 'n' rollers (who might be equally well known today as the father of eighties songstress Kim). Plant, incidentally, was reportedly mortified when he discovered that "Sea of Love" was his biggest-selling single ever.

Fast-forward eighteen years, and that other all-covers package, *Dreamland*, took the same journey even further, as he set down more-or-less definitive retreads of "Morning Dew" and "Hey Joe"—songs that common wisdom already insisted had been done to perfection already, by acts (Jeff Beck and Jimi Hendrix, respectively) who had once vied furiously for Zeppelin's own Kings of Rock crown, but which Plant had already made a claim on, when he led the fabulous Zeppelin Convention jam team through them both, that fabulous night back in September 1970.

Now and Zen, **Manic Nirvana**, **Fate of Nations**, **Mighty Rearranger**—nine albums in twenty-four years is not exactly an exhaustive workload, but (and this is one lesson he did learn from Led) when it's quality, not quantity, that matters most, it's refreshing to know you can put on any one of Plant's solo albums, be it early, mid or recent, secure in the belief that it's going to be great. Indeed, *Mighty Rearranger*, Plant's most recent release at the time of *Nine Lives*, rounded out the box with no less aplomb and attack than the *Pictures* that opened it.

Truly, it's projects like this that give box sets a good name. Well, a better name than "epitaph," anyway.

While Plant lived out his post-Zeppelin career in livid limelight—at the same time, for all intents and purposes, doing whatever he felt like—bandmates Jimmy Page and John Paul Jones embraced only the latter part of that equation. They did what they wanted, but not many people were watching.

For Page, the 1980s in particular drifted past in a flurry of barely satisfactory dilettante doodlings, beginning with the less-than-stellar score to *Death Wish II*. No, not even the original movie. The sequel. He was in on the ground floor of Plant's Honeydrippers project, playing at the Atlantic Records party concert that was the band's first-ever performance; he cut that stellar LP with Roy Harper, *Whatever Happened to Jugula?*; and there was a stab at a supergroup, the distinctly infirm the Firm, which paired him with former Free/Bad Company frontman Paul Rodgers in a quartet certain elements of the media promptly dubbed Bad Zeppelin.

There would be two Firm albums, with the uninspired second demanding a revised insult as well (Even Worse Zeppelin, perhaps). And the sneaking suspicion that, far more than Plant missed Page, Page was missing Plant, was made evident when the real thing reconvened for a brief Live Aid blowout.

It does not seem to have been an overly joyous occasion. John Bonham's sad absence was filled by something called Phil Collins (bassist Tony Thompson and Plant's then-current guitarist Paul Martinez completed the lineup), and three songs split the Philadelphia night: "Rock and Roll," "Whole Lotta Love," and an inevitable "Stairway to Heaven." But alone of the armies that made that concert happen, Zeppelin declined to incorporate footage of their set into the souvenir DVD package because, said the ubiquitous official spokesman, it wasn't up to their usual standards. But what does that really mean? That they played like crap? Or that it wouldn't sound good in a car commercial?

In fact, Zeppelin's performance is well worth hunting down, if only to see the sheer joy on the faces of the three surviving members, and there were high hopes the reunion might become somehow permanent. For a while, anyway. But it quickly became apparent that the members had other fish to fry, and so Page marched on.

There was an appallingly ill-advised union with another seventies veteran, former Deep Purple and Whitesnake frontman David Coverdale, and in the midst of all this, just two albums where you could say Jimmy Page was really being true to his heritage: 1988's **Outrider**—his first and (at the time of this writing) only solo album; and a surprisingly enjoyable live hookup with **the Black Crowes**—themselves such a hot Xerox of old Free B-sides that the very fact **Live at the Greek** did not sound like a Firm reunion was enough to redeem it in many fans' eyes.

Outrider is especially worthy of investigation. According to reports at the time, Page was originally intending a double album, only for his plans to be destroyed when burglars broke into his home and made off, among other things, with his demo tapes. Insult was added to injury when these tapes then leaked out onto the bootleg market, and Page's enthusiasm for the project took a major knock there and then.

Still he persevered. Robert Plant came in for one track, the cowritten "The Only One," and John Bonham's son **Jason Bonham** made his recorded debut on the set. Page's old Immediate Records ally Chris Farlowe turned up as vocalist, and so did **John Miles**, a British singer-songwriter whose reputation (sadly or not) is largely built around a monstrous mid-1970s hit called **"Music,"** how it was both his first love and his last, music of the future, music of the past, et cetera, et cetera. At the time, a few voices compared the single's vast soundscape of shifting patterns and melodies with something Led Zeppelin might have turned out, and while it's highly unlikely that's why Page recruited Miles, still it was fun to hear how such a development might have turned out.

The Black Crowes union, on the other hand, was nothing short of a wild celebration, two nights at the Greek Theatre in Los Angeles that drew their contents from three principal sources: the old blues both Page and the Crowes had taken for their own; the Led Zeppelin catalog; and the Crowes' own repertoire. Which makes the ensuing record company politicking that removed the last from the album look even more like sour accountant-fueled grapes than it was probably meant to be.

No matter. Just as he had on the *Outrider* tour, Page threw open doors that led all the way back to the Yardbirds, and a sense-shaking assault on "Shapes of Things." **B.B. King**'s "Woke Up This Morning" and Willie Dixon's "Mellow Down Easy" were both in on the action, and so was a tribute to two of Britain's own greatest purist blues guitarists, **Jeremy Spencer** and Peter Green, the electrifying leads who powered the original Fleetwood Mac to such heights around the same time Zeppelin was first taking flight.

"Shake Your Money Maker" was an **Elmore James** blues that Spencer made his own on Mac's eponymous debut LP; "Oh Well" was that slice of pensive self-examination that marked the end of Green's tenure with the band in 1970.

But the heart of the beast was the Zeppelin catalog, revisited and revitalized with such panache that even the distinctly unsettling shrieks with which frontman Chris Robinson treated the tumultuous blues drawn from the backpack felt right. Music like this should not be ossified, locked into its own time and place, and sacrosanct among even its creators. Not every Zeppelin devotee will appreciate the Black Crowes' sometimes heavy-handed approach. But like the Queen nuts who sat through the aforementioned Paul Rodgers's union with that band's rump, you cannot fault the musicians' own need to continue playing the songs that made their name.

If Jimmy Page's output has been patchy, then John Paul Jones's post-Zeppelin meanderings have been just that—meanderings that rarely even glance in the direction of his past, although truly critical listeners might also acknowledge he was not exactly the most reliable force in Led Zeppelin, either. Certainly, few people who sat through his keyboard solos on the 1975 American tour will go out of their way to contradict author Stephen Davis's assertion, in the memoir *LZ-'75*, that some nights saw him sink into "the most banal clichés of the cocktail lounge pianist." It was no surprise, then, that the 1985 soundtrack that reunited Jones with Jimmy Page for the first time in five years was called *Scream for Help*. Because it was aptly titled.

However, like Page, perhaps Jones was simply saving up the best for his own solo debut, while allowing the 1980s and 1990s to pass in a frenetic flurry of session work. It would be the dedicated fan indeed who tracked down every album that gave Jones a credit during this period, as he returned to his 1960s roots and worked across the musical spectrum. But Peter Gabriel, R.E.M., Brian Eno, **the Mission** and **Heart**, Ben E. King, Lenny Kravitz, Diamanda Galas, **Foo Fighters**, and Butthole Surfers all benefited from his presence, and when 1999 finally stirred him into making a statement of his own, he left nobody in doubt as to why it had taken so long.

It was because, "When you've been in the best band in the world..."

It was heavier than a concrete balloon, this *Zooma*, songs cast in sandblasted granite blocks. "I walk a lot, that's where a lot of the riffs and ideas come from," Jones said at the time, and you could see what he meant. Skyscapes and seashapes emerged unbidden from the noise, and he was thrilled that the album caught many people, even longtime fans, completely by surprise.

"I think people think of me as quiet, maybe they expected an album of orchestral music, and long synthesizer pieces. But I wanted an album I could take on the road and wave in people's faces." And with a band that was definitely going to wave *something* at you—guitarist Nick Beggs was best known from eighties pop mayflies Kajagoogoo—that was a promise one couldn't take too lightly.

Of course, he knew Beggs was an odd choice for collaborator, even if Jones had his fair share of working with teenybop idols in the past: Herman's Hermits for one; his own good self for another, when Andrew Oldham contemplated launching the fresh-faced young Capricorn at a weeny, screamy audience.

But the once too-shy guitarist came with the highest recommendations, Jones said: "I didn't want any conventional guitars on the record, but I did want guitar sounds and feels, so I used Trey Gunn on touch guitar, and I was hoping he'd be able to come on the road with me. But his King Crimson commitments came first, so I asked Robert Fripp if there was anyone else he knew who'd work, and he suggested Nick."

It was a combination that spread itself generously over the U.S. that fall, an outing that marked Jones's first tour since an excursion with that other unlikely partnership, goth chanteuse Diamanda Galas, earlier in the decade. But the tapes that emerged from those performances proved the live show with Galas was as intense as the album. Jones promised beforehand that "we probably will play some old songs, the ones people want to hear." But not, he insisted, necessarily the ones they were shouting for.

"One night on the Diamanda tour, there was somebody in the audience called out for 'Kashmir,' or something. And Diamanda just fixed them with a glare, shot something back at them, a fuck you or something, and you could see the whole crowd just parting around this poor guy, leaving him standing on his own in the middle of the floor."

Somewhat cruelly, John Paul Jones chuckled at the memory. But when you've been in the best band in the world, you can afford to.

Soundgarden, circa 1990s. (Photofest)

9

A WORLD IN THEIR OWN IMAGE:
ZEPPELIN FRIENDS AND IMITATORS

The problem with being the biggest rock 'n' roll band in the world (and quite possibly the best, although the Stones and the Who might take exception to that) is that everybody wants a piece of you. And not only the fans. Other bands dissect your music in search of that magical single ingredient that will raise them from half-hopers to surefire smashes, and lazy critics will always reach first for your name when looking to compare some aspiring new act to something familiar.

This was not so much of a problem during the 1970s; the media were still too engrossed in seeking out "the new Jimi Hendrix" to overly exert themselves finding a "new Led Zeppelin" as well. And more hopeful young guitarists were spiked by having to live up to that "honor" than we ever want to count.

At the same time, however, it is safe to say (and, even if it weren't, it would be said regardless) that Led Zeppelin did more to change the face of seventies rock than any other band. Not deliberately, and probably not even consciously. But at least across the course of their first four albums, and perhaps as late as their fifth and sixth, where Zeppelin led, a universe would follow, until the end of the decade saw their list of achievements embrace everything from the birth of heavy metal to the need for punk rock.

And it is true. Dig deep into the music of the age and Zeppelin's shadow was cast over so many souls that it became all too easy to dismiss a lot of them. Rather than praise a new band for its original elements, it was far easier to condemn them for those they had "borrowed." And few people ever even considered the fact that terming anything a "Zeppelin rip-off" was itself disingenuous, because Zeppelin themselves comprised so many different elements that they gladly acknowledged were drawn from elsewhere.

Watch the spectacular *The Song Remains the Same* movie, however, and one area that Zeppelin certainly did blast to prominence becomes instantly apparent. It's the area that, even with the best will in the world, many viewers will fast-forward through by the time they reach the third or fourth viewing.

Zeppelin made it de rigueur for musicians to play solos. Long solos. Endless solos. Solos that might, in a parallel universe, still be rumbling on now.

And the king of the solos was the drummer. John Henry Bonham.

Peter Grant, Led Zeppelin's manager throughout their career, once recalled the time John Bonham heard a joke. "We were at a party, and somebody came out with the one about 'What do you call a man who hangs with musicians? ... A drummer.' Bonzo walked over, towering above this guy, and asked, 'And what do you call a man who hangs with drummers?' Then he just picked the guy up and swung him over the balcony, about twenty floors above the ground." Grant laughed. "I never did hear the punch line, but I'm so glad the guy didn't say, 'Let me go.' Bonzo probably would have."

What was it about the sixties and seventies that spawned so many demented drummers? Once upon a time, the drummer was Mr. Rock Steady—Reliable Ringo, Charming Charlie, quietly spoken and turned-out gentlemen who would no sooner drive a limo into a swimming pool than they would take a ten-minute solo.

But then the worm turned. The Pretty Things' Viv Prince, the Who's Keith Moon, Bonzo Bonham—trace the line of descent far enough and you'll eventually wind up with *The Muppet Show*'s Animal, and that, maybe, is what finally put a stop to the entire process. A guitarist goes crazy and his admirers cite Pete

Townshend. A singer gets nutsy and he could be Iggy Pop. But a drummer? "Hey, man, you're just like the hairy one from the Muppets." When, in fact, there's a convincing school of thought that insists that Animal himself (itself?) was based on John Bonham.

Certainly Bonham was one of a kind. Less deliberately madcap than Moon, less unpredictably destructive than Prince, Bonham instead radiated an unspoken violence, a sense that, even in a good mood, you wouldn't really want to cross him. Peter Grant, himself no slouch when it came to safeguarding Zeppelin's various interests, had no compunction about bringing Bonzo along when things needed to be sorted out, and the more fraught those somethings were, the better Bonham liked it.

His bandmates were no less in awe of Bonzo than anybody else. According to legend, it was touch-and-go whether the Birmingham-born drummer would even join the band that became Led Zeppelin; he was touring the U.K. with American singer-songwriter Tim Rose at the time, earning forty pounds a night without having to break a sweat.

The fact that he was more or less untried at the time did not deter Jimmy Page. Indeed, the question he asked himself when he first saw Robert Plant perform—"What is wrong with this guy, that he's not already been snapped up by a star?"—must have echoed again when he first witnessed Bonham in full flood. Because Tim Rose was as good as it had got for the twenty-year-old drummer.

At school, Bonham's headmaster predicted the boy would end up either a dustman or a millionaire. The bands he'd played with so far at that point leaned toward the former—local club and pub acts that were most comfortable opening someone else's show, and only once bothered the world at large, when the Senators cut a single called "She's a Mod."

Birmingham natives both, Bonham and Plant first worked together in a local act called A Way of Life, and again in a new group, Band of Joy, a soul and blues outfit the singer formed in 1966, and which went through various incarnations before Bonham joined the following year.

BONHAM AND PLANT: THE BIRMINGHAM YEARS

THE SENATORS, "She's a Mod"/"I Know a Lot About You"
A super-rare single from 1964, also included (in an alternate, earlier version) aboard a period compilation album of local bands, *Brum Beat*, and the soundtrack to a movie called *Steppin' Out*. John Bonham's vinyl debut.

LISTEN, "You'd Better Run"/"Everybody's Gonna Say"
Dating from November 1966, Robert Plant's first-ever vinyl excursion, wrapping his not-yet-so-distinctive tonsils around a Young Rascals cover.

ROBERT PLANT, "Our Song"/"Laughin' Cryin' Laughin'"
A March 1967 solo single for Plant.

ROBERT PLANT, "Long Time Comin'"/"I've Got a Secret"
Robert Plant's second solo single, recorded with John Bonham and the Band of Joy in summer 1967.

ALEXIS KORNER, "Operator" (from the LP *Bootleg Him*)
Recorded in 1968 with the young Robert Plant on vocals.

Band of Joy cut a slew of demos in early 1968, but record company interest was less than zero and, by the spring of that year, the band had broken up. But they lightly touched a strand of their future when bassist Dave Pegg, later of Fairport Convention, joined the group briefly, and they made a great impression on Tim Rose when they toured behind him on his first visit to the U.K. So when Rose returned and found they'd broken up, he hired Bonham for his own band.

It took a lot of persuasion to pry Bonham away from that, but it was worth every plea, because, so integral to the eventual creation did he become that, when Bonham died, there was no question in anybody's mind that Zeppelin died with him. Not for them the protracted, tragic zombiehood that awaited Keith Moon's survivors in the Who. No less than in 1968, Zep without Bonzo was never even a contender, and you understood why every time you went to another stadium-rock show and heard the headliner's drummer undertake his own solo.

Bonzo was not the first rock drummer to consign a solo to wax. Cream, too, emphasized virtuosity in their music, with guitarist Eric Clapton and bassist Jack Bruce both enjoying their extended moment in the spotlight.

But it was Ginger Baker's tumultuous **"Toad"** that became the live show's signature, and that was a good couple of years before Bonham came along. So, no, Bonham wasn't the first drummer to give people an excuse to go the bar midshow. He was, however, the first to ensure that solos were a requisite weapon in every percussionist's arsenal.

From the moment Bonzo's "Moby Dick" showcase surfaced in Zeppelin's live set, expanding out of its relatively restrained vinyl (*Led Zeppelin II*) counterpart to consume fifteen, sometimes twenty minutes of the stage show, drummers who had not even grasped the basic elements of rhythm were suddenly miking up more drums than they could ever possibly reach, and walloping everything in sight.

It was a grotesque development, and Peter Grant once admitted that Bonzo himself resented it furiously. When he went to a live show, he wanted to be entertained and impressed. Most of the solos he found himself sitting through would have been laughed out of Zeppelin's rehearsal room. He never apologized for unleashing the plague in the first place, though, and why should he? Did Picasso say sorry every time another bad painter daubed his doodles on canvas? Did Peter O'Toole cringe when he first saw Tom Hanks?

There is good and bad in every endeavor, and Bonham was lucky enough that, because he was so good, he could afford to be really bad when he wanted to. He became the archetypal rock 'n' roll bad boy, fueled on the booze that would eventually kill him, but buoyant on his reputation regardless. And, it seemed, the more excess his onstage antics provoked among his peers, the more excessive his offstage behavior became.

Fight fire with fire. Genesis P-Orridge, art guerilla and industrial pioneer, recalls one night in the early 1970s when his band of the time found itself sharing the bill with a group whose own drummer prided himself on extended solos. Aghast at the arrogance of the musician in question, he suggested his own drummer out-extend every one.

"I told him to play a solo, and all the time, our roadie would be bringing out another drum, so the longer the solo lasted, the more drums he'd have to play it on." It sounds hilarious, but it also highlighted the downside of soloing. Some people just didn't know when to stop.

Carmine Appice of Vanilla Fudge was another percussive wizard, crashing around the kit with both abandon and purpose, and while that band was more or less finished by the time Led Zeppelin took flight, neither musicians nor audiences have ever forgotten the string of gigs they played together, as Zeppelin toured the U.S. for the first time. Now that *would* have been a sight to behold.

Patrick MacDonald, music critic for *The Seattle Times*, was at the pairing's show in that city in December 1968. He recalled, "Led Zeppelin was unknown—its debut album had not yet been released in America—and the audience almost completely ignored them. The house lights were not even turned down during their set, because so many people were still finding their seats. People talked over the music.

"It's one of the greatest shows I ever saw. The opening song, a cover of the blues classic 'Train Kept A-Rollin',' hit me so hard that I stood on my chair, waved my arms, and yelled and screamed. Somebody behind me said, 'Will you please sit down?' I turned and loudly pleaded, 'Didn't you hear that? Don't you get it? Shut up and listen!' Everybody around looked at me like I was nuts."

The joys of hindsight. Search for Zeppelin and Fudge together on the Internet and you will find testimonial after testimonial that claims "Zeppelin were amazing, I don't even remember Vanilla

Fudge." Even MacDonald, reflecting on the concert from a forty-years distance, refers to the evening's headliners as "now deservedly forgotten."

Phooey! Forget Vanilla Fudge and you forget one of the few contemporary bands that could give Zeppelin a run for their musical money, not only in terms of virtuosity, but also in terms of influencing a whole new generation to arise in their image.

It is the live Fudge experience the Zeppelin fan should familiarize himself with, and thankfully, there's more than enough to go 'round, splattered across fully fifty percent of the band's *Box of Fudge* box set.

True, you need to be in a very particular mood to digest this package in one sitting, for the Fudge themselves demanded it. Not for them the simple conventions of song and performance. If a chorus could be taken off in unforetold directions, if an intro could be expanded to the length of other people's albums, or if a solo could be draped with more excess baggage than a planeload of kleptomaniacs, the Fudge not only knew how to do it, they'd already rehearsed it to perfection. And that was in the studio. Live, Vanilla Fudge did not just redefine self-indulgence—they made it their own.

Ah, but they were brilliant as well, which is why the four discs here rate so highly. Two discs round up the band's "official" studio output, hitting every high point that has to offer; two more delve into the archive in search of eleven live cuts from a New Year's Day 1969 Fillmore show; and yes, "Season of the Witch" is here, in all the glory it ought to radiate.

But the oft-covered, multicolored Donovan composition is not even the peak of their endeavors. There is their epic restatement of the Supremes' **"You Keep Me Hanging On,"** extended to three times its expected length and slowed to a traffic jamming crawl. There were signature reinventions of the Beatles' **"Ticket to Ride"** and the Zombies' **"Time of the Season."** And there were their own epic compositions too, convoluted masterstrokes of lurid sound and livid energy that knew no musical boundaries, and would not have acknowledged their existence if they had.

The closest any British band came to the Fudge was **Deep**

Purple—in fact, keyboard player Jon Lord admits it was seeing Fudge live and lurid in all their baroque magnificence, when they visited the U.K. in 1967, that inspired him to form Purple in the first place. And so it was that the first three Purple albums were very much cut in a similar mold. Who knew the Beatles' "Help" could last so long?

By the time vocalist Ian Gillan and bassist Roger Glover joined in 1969, however, the band was embracing a more riff-conscious, rock-heavy ethos, with guitarist **Ritchie Blackmore**—who grew up in much the same hotbed of London session work as Jimmy Page (and also played with Screaming Lord Sutch)—following his old friend into the realms of guitar heroics.

But it was drummer Ian Paice who set the pace, with his personal showcase "The Mule" not only becoming a genuine highlight of the band's live show, but also making an even rarer transition to vinyl when it devoured great swaths of Purple's *Made in Japan* live album.

Zeppelin fans have always complained that the greatest live band of the 1970s needed to wait until the 2000s before being granted the live album they deserved, the so-stellar *How the West Was Won*. Purple fans might have the opposite complaint: that, although the group's discography is now swimming in live recordings, the very first one they ever released is the only one you truly need to complete your life.

Immaculately recorded across three nights of unbridled hysteria, and still home to the definitive versions of so many Deep Purple classics, *Made in Japan* perhaps received the ultimate accolade when the band drew the live rendition of the thunderous **"Smoke on the Water"** out as a single, and emerged with Deep Purple's biggest U.S. hit since their Fudged-up assault on "Hush" in 1968. "Smoke on the Water" billowed into the Top Five in 1973, and when, two years later, Purple themselves compiled their first best-of collection, *24 Carat Purple*, that steaming version of "Smoke" was joined by two more cuts from the live album, **"Strange Kind of Woman"** and **"Child in Time."** The radio-friendlier studio versions didn't even get a look in.

That is the company "The Mule" was keeping, and that was the rarified stratum to which it so successfully aspired. Other bands, however, were less fortunate in the percussive spotlight, and it is informative to note that, of all the groups who could be considered Zeppelin's rivals for the hard-rock throne during the first half of the 1970s, Purple alone can be remembered for matching "Moby Dick." Of the others—Britain's Black Sabbath and Uriah Heep; Americans **Grand Funk Railroad** and, laughably, **Kiss**; the Netherlands' **Golden Earring**; and Canadians **Rush** and (okay, they're from Seattle, but they got their start in Canada) Heart—few folk, if any, wax nostalgic for the solos. It was the riffs, the moods, the songs that swung, and darting through the catalogs of all those bands and more, those are the things that still resonate today.

If Black Sabbath had never existed, somebody would have been forced to invent them. They were never Satanists, or any of the other things misguided parents and preachers complained; rather, they adopted the imagery in the hope that the same people who lined up to see the latest horror movies might then line up to see them, and the fact that they succeeded so well had nothing to do with a pact with the Devil. Not unless you think good marketing is somehow aligned to witchcraft.

Good marketing and good music. For reasons that are still not totally clear, Sabbath quickly found themselves jousting with Led Zeppelin for supremacy in something called heavy metal, a musical genre whose parameters seemed to shift every time a new band turned the volume up (it would be the early 1980s before it truly fossilized around the stultifying clichés that now feed the beast). Certainly the two bands had little more than popularity in common: Zeppelin flourished because the song decidedly didn't remain the same; Sabbath soared because once guitarist Tony Iommi nailed a riff, it stayed nailed.

No less than *Led Zeppelin I*, Sabbath's eponymous debut was more a blueprint for what they *could* become than a definitive statement of who they were. Only the self-aggrandizing title track and the morbid dead weight of **"N.I.B."** truly posited directions the band would follow. But like Zeppelin, they found their feet fast.

Built around the leviathan riffery of **"Iron Man"** and the Vietnam protest **"War Pigs," *Paranoid*** (1970) was Sabbath's answer to *Led Zeppelin II*. So was ***Master of Reality*** (1971), and so was ***Volume Four*** (1972), making for a triptych of albums that blend into such a seamless whole, even the reinventions the band toyed with over successive LPs could not dismiss the sheer singularity of their formative vision. So Sabbath fell by the wayside a little with time, and by the time they broke up in 1978 (or, at least, replaced vocalist Ozzy Osbourne with the diminutive Ronnie James Dio), even diehards rarely mentioned their name in the same breath as Zeppelin's any longer.

That wasn't simply Sabbath's problem, though. The sad fact is, few of the groups who rode the metal horse to joust with Zeppelin truly lasted the pace—not through any deficiencies of their own (well, not always)—but because they missed the most intrinsic element of Zeppelin's alchemy: the fact that metal was simply one string on their bow, and a not especially well-plucked one, either.

The first band to truly comprehend this, and to run with it as well, was Queen, as guitarist Brian May happily acknowledges. The infant Queen regularly included *Led Zeppelin III*'s "Gallows Pole" in their live show, so when the first critical notices lumped them into the glam-rock bag (stop laughing at the back; it's true!), May noted, "it was extremely frustrating because we were already ...there was no such thing as glam rock back [when we started], we were just a band who liked theatrics. We thought of ourselves as a kind of Led Zeppelin who enjoyed dressing up. By the time things started happening, though, people like Sweet and Slade, great pop groups who were also dressing up, were huge and what we originally thought of as a very original approach was suddenly the latest fashion."

It was not a role the band themselves relished. "Fashion, movements, really don't matter when you're a band, all you care about is what's inside you and you really don't want to be fit into somebody's box. I'd much rather spend time finding out what the differences are between people than looking for the similarities."

Not that Queen made any conscious efforts to shake off the

unwanted baggage, May continued, "mainly because we were much too arrogant and pigheaded to care." Indeed, the sophisticated decadence of 1974's **Sheer Heart Attack**, and, in particular, the **"Killer Queen"** single, so effortlessly fit the mood of the time that even today, the song is a deathless regular in glam revivalist circles.

But May is equally adamant that that, too, was utterly unpremeditated. "We just did what we thought was worthwhile; there really was a terrible arrogance about us! But what that really means is, you're creating from the inside, rather than from an opinion poll. We never considered what people were saying as a guide to what we were doing. It doesn't mean we didn't care about our audience, because we cared deeply about them. But caring about your audience doesn't mean doing what they want you to do. It means treating yourself properly as an artist, so you are worthy of people's support. And if you're acting with integrity within yourself, your audience will understand that."

That integrity took the band down some remarkable roads, of course. Six minutes of rock, opera, and anything else they could throw into the pot, **"Bohemian Rhapsody"** is merely the tip of an iceberg of almost Brobdingnagian creativity, audacity, and, as May insists, arrogance. You can stop off on any one of Queen's albums to touch similarly scintillating heights, but for the full effect of Queen at the peak of their musical daredevilry, the first four albums are the place to start: **Queen I** and **Queen II**, so named to further the Zeppelin link, of course; the aforementioned *Sheer Heart Attack*; and **A Night at the Opera**.

Queen's own roots in the blues, shared with Led Zeppelin of course, were rarely as pronounced as Zep themselves allowed theirs to be. But one song, the B-side to **"Seven Seas of Rhye,"** their first hit single, is compulsive and compulsory listening if you want to spot the moment where the two bands both united and then diverged.

"See What a Fool I've Been," as May said, "was a little bit out of the scope of our main thrust," but also "it really represented us onstage in the early days, doing bluesy things which was a lot of fun." He continued: "From the beginning, we knew fairly clearly what our direction was, although it was argued about all the time. We always went for the maximum color and experiment and scope and breadth, and things like 'See What a Fool' didn't really belong in that.

"In fact, it was an adaptation of an existing blues standard— you're going to ask me which one, and I don't know! I heard it on a TV broadcast, it was one of those things where ...I remember hearing how the Beatles heard [the Shadows'] 'Apache' on the radio and wanted to do a version of it, but they weren't able to remember it properly, so they put together an instrumental which became 'Cry for a Shadow.' It was the same sort of thing. I heard this song once on a TV program and remembered about a third of it, and put together something which, in my mind, is the same thing. And I don't know how much accurately I did it because I still haven't found the original! It's funny, we were actually looking a few weeks ago to see if we could discover what the song was, and who the original author was. I'd love to find out, because I'd like to pay the guy!"

Now there's a thought.

So that's the early days. But Queen's entire career—a seventeen-year span that halted only with the tragic death of singer Freddie Mercury—is pocked with equivalent classic songs, including one that even traveled back to their first shows, by reiterating the clarion call of "Immigrant Song."

"Flash," the theme to the movie of almost the same name (Dino De Laurentiis's *Flash Gordon*) might well be the greatest tribute Led Zeppelin have ever been paid, all the more so since the tribute itself was buried beneath so much of Queen's own self-effacing bombast that scarcely anyone even noticed it.

Brian May recalls the song's gestation. "Really, there had never been a rock soundtrack to a movie that wasn't about rock music before; up to that point, it was considered impossible. Even Mr. De Laurentiis said it'd never work. It was Mike Hodges, the producer, who brought us in to the project, and I think there was a fundamental gap between his view of the film and Mr. De

Laurentiis's; Mike Hodges really made it into a cult film by being very self-consciously kitsch, whereas Dino regarded it as an epic, and not to be messed with.

"I'll never forget, he came to the studio, sat down and listened to our first demos, and said, 'I think it's quite good, but the theme will not work in my movie, it is not right.' And Mike walked over and said, 'A chat with you, Dino. You don't understand where this film is going to be pitched.' But I had a really nasty moment there: 'Oh, no, he hates my "Flash, aaaahh-aaaaaahhh," and it's going to go on the cutting room floor.'"

Instead, it left that land of ice and snow and became one of the most beloved movie themes in history. And why? Because it looked at whatever bag Queen's fans and foes insisted their music fell into, and made certain it wriggled out again, and it's that more than anything else that so readily aligns Queen with Zeppelin.

Go on, name five Zeppelin songs that actually adhere to the tenets of true heavy metal. "Whole Lotta Love," if you take out the sound effects. "Rock and Roll" and "Black Dog," if you overlook the fact that the album where they came from (*Led Zeppelin IV*) was perhaps the group's most eclectic yet. "Trampled Under Foot," because it had a riff to die for, but which was really just funked-up Chuck Berry. And "Heartbreaker." Maybe.

Now name the songs that *weren't* metal, and you start to put yourselves in the same headspace that two Pacific Northwesterly–based sisters found themselves in, as they started putting together their own band in 1973 or so. Heart might as well have started as a Zeppelin tribute band, so many covers were crushed into the two-girl, three-guy lineup's early repertoire. But it was the Zeppelin of "The Battle of Evermore," "Stairway to Heaven," and "Kashmir" that excited Ann and Nancy Wilson's ears, and Heart's debut album, 1976's **Dreamboat Annie**, did not emerge merely one of the greatest North American debut albums of the 1970s. It is also, thanks to the sheer strength of the band's original material (**"Magic Man"** and **"Crazy on You"** both lurk within), one of the precious few albums that can stand up in front of a crowd and say, "Yeah, I like Led Zeppelin. SO WHAT?"

Touring their debut across the USA in summer 1976, Zeppelin remained a touchstone for Heart, no matter how snippy the occasional critics got. Their version of "Battle of Evermore" was stellar, "The Rover" was surprising, and "Rock and Roll" was of course a ginormous set opener that established the Wilson sisters as the hottest hard-rock female outfit since the primal days of **Fanny**—themselves a band whose acknowledgment of Zeppelin twisted as far from the Heart model as it was possible to get (the quartet were more prone to covering the Beatles and Marvin Gaye), but buoyant regardless in their refusal to stay in one musical place.

Neither was Heart's debut a fluke. *Little Queen*, the band's second album, took the same template to even greater extremes, not only serving up two bona fide riff-rock anthems, **"Barracuda"** and the title track, but also out *III*-ing *Led Zeppelin III* with **"Sylvan Song"** and **"Dream of the Archer."** Add the live cover of "Stairway to Heaven" that surfaced among *Little Queen*'s CD bonus tracks in 2004, and Heart's heart would never beat so proudly again. It did not need to—by the time of 1978's *Dog and Butterfly*, they had written the song that more or less stands as the "Stairway" for the 1980s, "Mistral Wind."

Established now among the most successful hard-rock bands of the American decade, Heart never lost, or forgot, their own personal grasp of their musical past, points that were made with the **Lovemongers** side project in 1992. A live EP included a sensational return to "The Battle of Evermore" and, when the Heart mothership regrouped in 1995, it was to cut a live acoustic set with producer (and special guest multi-instrumentalist) John Paul Jones: the lovely *The Road Home*, blistered with unplugged renderings of many of the songs that set them on their course in the first place. Even more recently, a limited-edition run of the band's *Strange Euphoria* box set included a five-song mini-album called *Zeppish*, packed with five great Zep covers.

Heart were the epitome of bands that took the Led Zeppelin template in the seventies, and then ran it in directions that were wholly their own. But they were also one of the last to do it, at least for a short time. More or less simultaneous with Heart's breakthrough, the music scene in general was both riven and polarized by the punk-rock movement, bellowing from the twin points of New York and London and effectively removing any attempt to rehash rock's recent past from the menu.

It was a cosmetic break more than a cultural one, of course, and neither side of the divide was truly, lastingly, averse to one another's musical ventures. For Led Zeppelin and their generation, punk was very much a return to the same ethics of youth, volume, and temperament that had fired their own first musical efforts (with the added "bonus" of an instant media spotlight); and for the younger crowd—well, they all *liked* to say they'd spent their formative years imbibing an exclusive diet of the Stooges, the Velvet Underground, and the MC5, but if that was true, then all three would have sold a lot more records than they ever did. And punk would have had to react against *them*.

Gaye Advert of first-generation punkers the Adverts recalls her band rehearsing in the same London studio as Led Zeppelin in late 1976, conducting auditions while various members of the Zeppelin dropped in to say hello and ask how things were going. At least one prospective percussionist was so overwhelmed by the sight of the superstars standing in the doorway, watching while he set up his kit, that he promptly fled the building.

It wasn't long after that that Robert Plant, John Bonham, and Jimmy Page showed up at the Roxy, London's premier punk niterie, to catch one of the Damned's Monday night residencies. John Bonham even got up to jam with them, or would have if the venue's management hadn't mistaken him for a fat, abusive drunk and thrown him offstage, while Plant and Page laughingly looked on. His last words as he was pulled onto the dance floor were "This is a fucking great band," and when Plant was asked later if bands like the Damned and the Adverts reminded him of his own early days, he denied it. They reminded him, he said, of Led Zeppelin's most recent rehearsal.

Still, you will look far and wide for any overt punk tributes to Led Zeppelin, with the one that most ears would recognize, California speed-punks the Dickies' breakneck rendering of "Communication

Breakdown," better regarded as a novelty than a true musical tip of the hat.

At the same time, however, there was an undercurrent that had learned its trade at Zeppelin's knee, and although the U.K. media pointedly failed to acknowledge it, many of the clubs that gave a welcome first break to a new punk band also extended similar privileges to the harbingers of another, concurrent, movement— the metallic clash of what would soon become known (so unfortunately) as the New Wave of British Heavy Metal.

Today, the NWoBHM is best remembered for the mere brace of true future superstars who emerged from it, **Def Leppard** and **Iron Maiden**. At its 1979–1980 peak, however, a small telephone directory could have been compiled around the insurgence of new talents, whose own musical influences ran the gamut of past heroes. Led Zeppelin, Black Sabbath, and Deep Purple were simply the top of the pile.

Diamond Head, **Girlschool**, **Angel Witch**, **Magnum**, **Saxon**, **Tank**, **Praying Mantis**, **Tygers of Pan Tang**, **Samson**, **Witchfynde**, **Wrathchild**...between them, and many more besides, the NWoBHM not only reestablished metal as a viable musical force in the British (and, although it never truly faded, American) marketplace following the firestorms of punk, it also did much to revitalize the careers of bands who had either failed or been forgotten the first time around. Groups like **Atomic Rooster**, **Budgie**, and **Motörhead** all grasped the helping hands the NWoBHM extended; so did the likes of **Gillan** and **Whitesnake**; and though the ensuing morass can only tangentially be tied to any direct Zeppelin input, guitarist **John Du Cann** of Atomic Rooster spoke for many when he said: "Zeppelin's influence was greatest in the fact that it was not obvious.

"Because that was how they did it. You knew where their influences lay, but you couldn't listen to 'Kashmir' or 'Trampled Under Foot' and say, 'Ah, they've been listening to so-and-so.' That's what guided the best of the New Wave of British Heavy Metal." It is, therefore, what has guided the best of metal since then, and no matter that the likes of **Guns N' Roses** (Budgie, tarred and feathered), **the Killers** (Deep Purple without the color), **Metallica** (Sabbath after the shops all closed), and so forth have all risen up singing the praises of the originators. The fact is that the best metal keeps its mouth shut and lets its own originality do the talking.

And so it was that it would be another half decade before a true successor to the Zeppelin *sound* came along, and it appeared from the most unexpected angle yet. Britain's gothic-rock scene, after all, is notoriously shrouded in darkness and mist, in rattling chains and sepulchral voices, and the incessant, if somewhat obvious, observation that Bela Lugosi is dead.

Yet from the wreckage of perhaps the hoariest of all the original bands on the scene, the three-man/one-drum-machine Sisters of Mercy, there arose a new group who didn't simply want to sound like Led Zeppelin. They brought in a producer who would make damned certain that they did.

Guitarist Wayne Hussey's the Mission had already scored one hit single, "Stay with Me," and a Top 20 debut album, *God's Own Medicine*, when they set about planning their most definitive statement, and the speed with which they had risen up both the charts and the gig circuit left few people denying that, as 1987 came to an end, the Mission were poised to become one of the biggest bands of the age. *Children* was the album that would confirm those prophecies.

The album sessions were slow and painstaking. The Mission knew what was at stake, knew they were expected to construct an album that would not only consolidate, but confirm, all their debut had promised. Yet they also had a secondary agenda, one that kept the band members smiling long into the night, probably as they leafed through a scrapbook of bad-tempered cuttings-so-far that were united in one harsh criticism: that the Mission were little more than a reconstructed Led Zeppelin, as prone to musical hyperbole and symbolic meaninglessness as that most hairy of hallowed pre-punk dinosaurs.

There was just one thing to do. They invited John Paul Jones along to produce the sessions.

It was a cautious courtship. The Mission had approached Jones the moment they heard he was considering widening his own horizons to begin working with "new" bands. Jones, however, was not at all keen, first experiencing the band through their press coverage and then, having recanted slightly after hearing *God's Own Medicine*, being utterly underwhelmed when he caught them in concert, opening for U2 at one of that band's British football stadium congregationals in summer 1987.

Finally agreeing to meet the Mission, Jones rapidly changed his mind again; meeting Jones, the Mission in turn reversed their entire perspective on studio work. Tim Palmer, producer of their debut, had been content to let the band record as fast and frenzied as they wished. Jones, on the other hand, had a meticulous touch that could let days be spent trying to perfect the most minute element of a song.

The Mission acceded to his every command. Only Jones's reservations about the band's continued indulgence in amphetamines, scarcely a drug suited to such an agonizing approach, rattled the composure of the sessions, and, when *Children* was finally released in March 1988 (on the heels of the hymnal "Tower of Strength" single), it was clear the new approach had worked. Still recognizably the Mission, still a florid flourish of smirking gothic cliché and unashamed seventies rock excess, *Children* emerged among the very best albums that Led Zeppelin never made—in the very best sense of the phrase.

It was vast, a symphonic rock experience that surely reached its peak with the latest in the band's always well-chosen catalogue of covers, American hard-rock giants **Aerosmith**'s **"Dream On,"** and via a closing number that, as if the rest of the message was not hard-hitting enough, addressed the Mission's ambitions with neon clarity.

Riding a riff that could have been cut from **the Cult** (another nominally goth crew whose ears had never strayed far from a Zeppelinesque example), shotgun-wedded to the galloping rhythm of Zeppelin's own "Immigrant Song," opening the verse with a stadium-shaking yelp, then throwing in a primary-school choir for added anthemic piquancy, **"Hymn (for America)"** was so blatant as to be blinding, and all the more brilliant because of it. The Mission had made an album that felt like Led Zeppelin. Now it was time to find out if they flew like them—and, fleetingly, they did. *Children* was massive and, while the band is still a going concern today, *Children* remains the apex of their achievement. And what an apex it is.

Through the 1970s and into the 1980s, bands were compared to Zeppelin for direct musical reasons. Canadian horseheads Rush, for example, rose to massive peaks by virtue of combining the most florid bits of Zeppelin with the most floral elements of Yes, a plateau of self-indulgent pomposity only Styx came close to matching. But Randy Jackson's **Zebra** and Ronnie James Dio's pre-Rainbow outfit **Elf** both gnawed satisfyingly on the Zeppelin form book, with Zebra apparently starting life as the next best thing to a Zeppelin cover band before lurching into their own dimension.

A decade later, **Kingdom Come** took the comparisons even further, but like so many other bands, hamstrung their own chances of being seen as something more than a metal band (which is, of course, the prerequisite of any truly worthwhile Zeppelin photocopy) by not really stepping outside the genre. It would be the late 1980s/early 1990s before a wave of new bands emerged who did not so much emulate Zeppelin but actually assimilated them into their own sound, looking back over the full expanse of the group's catalog and drawing, whether consciously or not, more than a handful of elements into their own material, and using that as the foundation for the future—in much the same way, in fact, as Zeppelin took the blues and folk of their own adolescence, and transformed that into something that was all their own.

The Mission's *Children* certainly aided this quest, setting itself up as a starting point for any ears interested in tracing backwards. But it was **Jane's Addiction**, a somewhat disheveled post-gothic, post-punky and, to many ears, post-melodic art-rock outfit, who truly set the bar for the next decade.

In truth, there were few points upon which the two bands would have agreed. Like Robert Plant, Jane's frontman Perry Farrell had a very distinctive voice. But it was a nasal whine as opposed to a full-blooded shriek, and besides, Guns N' Roses had already made the sound of nails on a chalkboard their own. Similarly, while guitarist Dave Navarro certainly fit the bill for a modern-day guitar hero, his instrument was armed for noise more than nuance, and in the chaotic assault of an all-out Jane's performance, one would have expected to see him slicing his strings with an actual violinist, rather than a simple bow.

And yet.

Both **Blind Melon** and the Black Crowes rose from beds made to the strains of Jane's Addiction's more ambitiously tuneful moments—themselves largely contained to the band's first greatest hits collection, wherein such career highlights as "Jane Says" and "Been Caught Stealing" are wrapped around more elysian fare; indeed, we have already seen (in chapter seven) how the Black Crowes achieved official recognition of sorts when Jimmy Page joined them to record a live album together.

Blind Melon, on the other hand, sadly never had the opportunity to truly trace, or even shake off, the formative influences the critics claimed shone brightly, with the death of frontman Shannon Hoon cutting them down before they'd even cut a second album. Besides, being influenced by a band who might have been influenced by another band is scarcely the most direct line of aural descent. Especially when another group had already emerged who happily traced their own lineage back to late nights spent listening to Led Zeppelin albums, and maintained their story even after they were roped into another genre entirely.

Soundgarden, up there with Pearl Jam and Nirvana, hallmarked the so-called grunge sound of Seattle, a maverick musical roar that owed as much to its geographical confines—the overcast gray of the Pacific Northwest, and the fact that even big city Seattle still thinks like a forgotten logging community—as to any musical preferences. Metal, of course, was big in those parts, and Heart spent much of their formative time there, and so did Queensrÿche, for anybody who wants to remember them.

That's where grunge diverged from the standard MacRiffery of most local rock scenes, and that's how this one regional pinprick rose, in 1991, to become the most famous musical city in the world. Because grunge sounded like a lot of people felt: gray, hopeless, and permanently damp.

Soundgarden were always cut out to be different, however, as guitarist Kim Thayil explained. As a local DJ before the band got going, he aired the music he listened to at home—British post-goth'ers like Bauhaus, Joy Division, the first Psychedelic Furs album, and the Cure. The same backwash, in fact, that informed the Cult and the Mission.

"Those were the big influences on Soundgarden when we started," Thayil explained, while remembering how the band's early gigs were attended by the same white-faced goth girls who habitually grooved to Specimen and Sex Gang Children, and who found much the same magic lurking inside Soundgarden. "But we were also into the SST bands: Black Flag, the Minutemen, the Meat Puppets. The second Meat Puppets album changed my life."

But it is also true that the band turned down an opportunity (extended by Gene Simmons) to appear on a Kiss tribute album because, shuddered Soundgarden bassist Ben Shepherd, "his fans used to beat me up on the way home from school. I was into Led Zeppelin and things, which they all called 'older brother music,' so they beat me up." From the outset, then, Soundgarden's welding of British art-school neuroses and American punk psychoses, its sense of purpose strengthened by the other bands who emerged alongside them, was destined to ensure the band remained one of nineties rock's most misunderstood mutants.

"At the beginning, a lot of people thought we sounded like Led Zeppelin," Thayil continued, "mainly because we have a singer who can hit the high notes without sounding screechy." When Soundgarden were first picked up by the press, "that's what every writer compared us to, because that's what everyone had told them."

The band itself believed they'd "moved on." But the reviewers continued happily playing follow-the-leader, and it was probably not with tongue-withdrawn-from-cheek that Soundgarden continued to let the odd Zep sound float into their music, in much the same way, and for many of the same reasons, that Zeppelin used to allow the occasional borrowed blues riff to leap out of the mix. It made them laugh, and it made the critics mad. What better reasons could there be to do something?

Soundgarden would in fact be four albums old (five, if you count a compilation of early EPs) before they were finally comfortable in that skin, and it is no shock that the album they turned out to celebrate the moment remains their most enjoyable, varied, and honest. 1994's **Superunknown** is Soundgarden at their most complete and compelling, more willing to be weird, and, yes indeed, reviving the old Led Zep comparisons they had ducked out of almost a decade before.

Oozing unheard emotion, the record offered a sense of sonic dynamism quite at odds with the band's sludgy reputation. It was also at odds, according to frontman Chris Cornell, with most people's expectations: "It [was] the first one where we've not been self-conscious about what we were doing. In the past, we'd only record songs if everybody in the group liked them—this time, we ...allowed each other more freedom."

The sitar-fired "Half," one of two Ben Shepherd songs on the album, was a case in point. With buried vocals howling from atop a minaret, "Half" could not have been further from the Soundgarden brief if it tried.

Prior to *Superunknown*, Cornell confirmed, "there was a sense that we were playing what the audience wanted to hear, rather than what we wanted to do." From there on out, they felt they could do anything, and in that spirit of absolute freedom, Soundgarden embraced the comparisons that used to make them mad, and proved they could be a positive point. If the only band people can compare you to is one everybody else has failed to emulate, you have to be doing something right.

Because anyone can *sound* like Led Zeppelin. The White Stripes sound like Led Zeppelin if you've never really listened to either band, and just go by first impressions (and the fact that their first two albums could easily be outtakes from *Led Zeppelins I and II*). Foo Fighters sound like Led Zeppelin if your experience of the latter are the most radio-friendly parts of the *Mothership* compilation. And so on.

The important thing is to *feel* like Led Zeppelin, and so we come to the greatest Led Zeppelin impersonation of all, the one that everybody yearned for but no one expected, the one that musical dreams were made of, but which nightmares could have sprung from. Jimmy Page and Robert Plant's reunion as—what else? **Page and Plant**.

Led Zeppelin, circa 1975, with "The Starship." (Photofest)

10

PAGING MR. PLANT:
REUNIONS AND REPASTS

In 1994, Robert Plant and Jimmy Page reunited for the first time in fifteen years (Live Aid notwithstanding), to reassess the legacy of the band they once helmed to world domination. An *MTV Unplugged* performance, a studio album, and a world tour all resulted, and here's a scary thought for you: More years have now elapsed since **Unledded**, as this project was called, than the original Led Zeppelin spent together in the first place. And the music hasn't held up badly, either, even if it won't ever replace the original band in our affections. It wasn't supposed to, after all.

The basics: Reconvening to reinvent their back catalog with the array of largely esoteric instrumentation that immediately placed their endeavors into the world-music bag, but retaining the solid rock push of their original vision, Page and Plant conceived an enterprise that was vastly more successful than it could have been.

Zeppelin had never shied away from exotic and unusual music stylings, with the *Physical Graffiti* album in particular allowing them to experiment far from the rocking crowd. *Led Zeppelin IV* was at least conceived with the Indian subcontinent in mind, and *Houses of the Holy* went so far as to serve up a genuine reggae number, and one that deserved far better than the dreadful pun that became its title.

The fact that "D'yer Mak'er" predates every other significant white rocker's attempt to capture the Caribbean sound (Eric Clapton's "I Shot the Sheriff," generally regarded as the hit that set that ball rolling, was still a year away) adds to the adventure, all the

IF YOU LIKE LED ZEPPELIN...

more so since Zeppelin would then become the first white rock band to be successfully parodied by a reggae act, **Dread Zeppelin**, as opposed to the other way around. Dread Zeppelin's first couple of albums, at least, are an object lesson in making a good joke last, although anybody seeking out a more faithful tribute should visit **Eek-A-Mouse**'s 1991 *U-Neek*, with its own effective cover of "D'yer Mak'er."

"D'yer Mak'er," perhaps surprisingly, did not make the *Unledded* set list. Of those that did, the CD rendering of the original MTV show features fourteen tracks, including two that skipped the original television broadcast ("Rain Song" and "Wah Wah"). The ninety-three-minute DVD spreads to seventeen songs, plus a bonus rehearsal of "Black Dog," an interview, and some montage-style live footage. And, although you don't want to sit there saying, "They look a lot older than I remember," the fact is, they do. They sound it as well—"Since I've Been Loving You," one of those Zeppelin balladic balls-breakers that encompasses everything the band once did so well, suddenly sounded just a little tired and sorry for itself; "Kashmir," one of the original group's most evocative numbers, seemed fiddly and overarranged.

There were some magical moments, though. "Gallows Pole" was as triumphantly swinging as any song about a hanging ought to be, while "When the Levee Breaks" had a thrusting energy that really did turn back the years. The introduction of esoteric Middle Eastern instrumentation (among other sounds) allowed the duo to turn their attention to currents that always swirled beneath, but rarely broke through, the original quartet's musical surface, and the opportunity to reinvent so many old favorites with new eyes and ears was clearly one both musicians relished.

And so it proved when the two hit the road, and promptly provoked considerable startled headlines with their open invitation for the bootleggers to simply roll the tapes, generously acknowledging that it was going to happen anyway, so the least they could do was wave to one another.

One inevitable sea of self-inflicted CDs (or, more recently, downloads) later, it is perhaps easier to play favorites among the

150

ensuing recordings than it was at the time, when the hype was still howling and every new disc offered fresh promise and possibility. Of them all, then, the show at the Shark Tank in San Jose, California, captured on the two-CD *Simple Truth* bootleg is hard to improve upon.

Resurrecting songs even the original Zeppelin rarely if ever performed (the B-side "Hey Hey What Can I Do" being a case in point), Page and Plant's repertoire was never predictable. Traditional concert chest-beaters like "Since I've Been Loving You," "Kashmir," and "Dazed and Confused," of course, played their part in the set. But in a show whose prime intent was to reevaluate, rather than rehash Zeppelin's career, that also left room for "In the Evening," "Four Sticks," "Friends," and "No Quarter," that somewhat po-faced lowlight of *Houses of the Holy* that genuinely benefitted from John Paul Jones's absence.

There was also a nod toward drummer Porl Thompson's past with the Cure, a deliciously funereal plod through that band's eerie paean to arachnophobia, **"Lullaby,"** and while we're on the subject of unexpected moments, look out for a copy (audio or video) of Page and Plant's appearance on Australian TV's *The Money or the Gun*.

THE MONEY OR THE GUN:
IS THAT A BUSTLE IN YOUR HEDGEROW,
OR ARE YOU JUST GLAD TO SEE ME?

Longtime Zep fans will be well aware of the premise of the show: it is a surreal musical outing whose guests are routinely forced to perform their own interpretation of "Stairway to Heaven." An album of the greatest renditions, sensibly titled *Stairway to Heaven*, was released in 1992, including distinctive and occasionally excruciating versions by such Aussie TV staples as Kate Ceberano and the Ministry of Fun, "Love Is in the Air" hitmaker John Paul Young, Pardon Me Boys, the Australian Doors Show and a B-52's tribute act called the Rock Lobsters, Sandra Hahn and Michael Turkic, an Elvis impersonator, the Beatnix, Vegemite

Reggae, and Leonard Teale. And veteran comedian/singer/artist **Rolf Harris**, who rendered the song in the spirit of his own "Tie Me Kangaroo Down, Sport" and was promptly rewarded with a U.K. Top 10 hit.

For Page and Plant to have honored the show with their own version of a song they already performed every night would, of course, have been futile. So host Andrew Denton offered them an even bigger challenge: Pay tribute to Rolf Harris instead. He bade them play Harris's **"Sun Arise"** ("My favorite!" laughed Plant), and no matter that the song had already received a rock treatment once before, when Alice Cooper covered it on 1971's *Love It to Death*—still it was an absolutely unexpected, and utterly priceless, moment.

Page and Plant reunited was first and foremost a live experience, a glorious consummation of two talents that should never have parted so soon—for remember, it was the death of John Bonham that ended Led Zeppelin, not the artistic, personal, or musical differences that normally sever a talent. And, as such, it brought an entire new generation into the arms of an act they had never had the opportunity to witness in the past. What it did *not* do, and neither was it intended to, was restart the career that had been so tragically curtailed.

True, a studio LP did emerge, ***Walking into Clarksdale***, but, perhaps fittingly, one listened in vain for more than the occasional spectral echo of past Zeppelin heights. Despite boasting no fewer than twelve brand-new songs composed by Page, Plant, and drummer Michael Lee (thirteen songs on the Japanese release), it is easier to file the disc away with the rest of Robert Plant's solo career, a mood he seems to share. Why else, a little more than a decade later, would he have revisited the best track on the original album, the keening "Please Read the Letter," during his collaboration with Alison Krauss? And how else could that pair have produced a far more fitting reading of the song than he did with the guitarist with whom he'd once straddled the universe?

Which is not to say *Walking into Clarksdale* should be avoided.

Combining the world-musical eclecticism of the live show with the contemporary rock stylings of producer du jour Steve Albini (fresh from nailing Nirvana's swan song, *In Utero*), *Walking into Clarksdale* could be seen as an attempt to bring the Zeppelin sound into the mid-1990s, and, as such, it succeeds. The question it did not answer, for reasons that should be obvious, was whether the Zeppelin sound *needed* to be brought there; or whether its original form was timeless enough that any move to modernize it would ultimately wind up sounding hollow and, incredibly, dated—complaints that could never be leveled at the original act. Particularly at a time when new bands like Foo Fighters and **Garbage** were rising to at least keep a Zeppelinesque spirit of adventure alive and kicking.

And so to the last official sighting of Led Zeppelin, touching down on the stage of London's O2 Arena on December 10, 2007, a benefit concert for their old Atlantic Records label head's Ahmet Ertegun Education Fund.

It was, as the headlines screamed on either side of the event, the first time Page, Plant, and Jones (plus John Bonham's son Jason) had set foot onstage together since Live Aid, more than two decades earlier, and their first full live performance since 1980. And no matter how high, or low, the onlooker's expectations, this was one of those shows that rose beyond criticism, buoyed on such an incredible wave of anticipation, excitement, and even gratitude that, even listening back to the inevitable bootlegs of the night, whether audio vérité digital recordings or rough snatches of fuzz through a cell phone microphone, it was impossible to come back to earth.

Reviewers simply listed the songs played, and let their drool stains serve as punctuation. Audience members gasped and looked 'round for news cameras to express their amazement to. And everyone who missed the shows hung hopefully to the rumors going round there'd be a few more shows in the new year.

There weren't, just as there were no officially sanctioned souvenir DVDs or live CDs. No less than at Live Aid, Led Zeppelin had come back together, in body, in soul, and in terms of quality control as well. Throughout the band's lifetime, and even in the face of what must be an overwhelmingly vociferous demand for the band members to return to the vaults and dig out something, anything, everything they ever taped and thrust them out for the public to devour, Led Zeppelin have never allowed their standards to dip. If something is going to be released beneath the band name, it had better be worthy of it.

Eight studio albums, plus one posthumous collection of outtakes.

One live movie soundtrack and, thirty years later, a two-CD/DVD live compilation.

A box set spanning the band's entire career, and a sort-of-greatest hits collection.

A slipcased collection of CD remasters.

And that's your lot.

If you like Led Zeppelin, you'll already have all of those.

So go back to page one—and try all of these too.

ACKNOWLEDGMENTS

Thanks to the usual cast of characters, suspects, and fictional beings for their assistance, advice, and enthusiasm as this book came to life, including: Amy Hanson, Jo-Ann Greene, Oliver, Toby and Trevor, Karen and Todd, Linda and Larry, Deb and Roger, Gaye and Tim, Dave and Sue, Bateerz and family, sundry gremlins, Barb East, Geoff Monmouth, and many more.

Gratitude, too, to my editor, Mike Edison, whose mastery of the bong guitar reduces me to daily paroxysms of awe; to my copy editor, Josh Wimmer; to my project editor, Jessica Burr; and to all at Backbeat.

And to the myriad Zeppelin peers, pals, disciples, and dreamers whose words and thoughts join mine in telling this story: John Paul Jones and the late Peter Grant, for interviews that touched some intriguing themes; and also, Alan Merrill, Carmine Appice, Mike Pinera, Jeff Beck, Brian May, Graham Gouldman, John Mayall, Alexis Korner, Jim McCarty, Daniel Gallagher, Peter Green, Mick Ralphs, Chris Cornell, Kim Thayil, Dave Walker, Dan McCafferty, Tony Iommi, Andrew Loog Oldham, Tony King, Tony Defries, Peter Noone, Lulu, Cliff Richard, and Gaye Advert.

Also to those who are no longer with us: John Entwistle, Mickie Most, John Du Cann, Noel Redding, Simon Kirke, Trevor Lucas, Tony Secunda, and Nico.

APPENDIX A:
FORTY LED ZEPPELIN COVERS
YOU WILL REALLY WANT TO HEAR

"ACHILLES LAST STAND"
Dream Theater never hid their love of Zeppelin under a bushel, meaning it's hard to pick any single cover out from a wealth of live recordings and say this is the band at its best. Their *A Change of Seasons* album does it for us, then, by medley-fying "Achilles" with "The Rover" and "The Song Remains the Same," recorded in London in 1995.

"ALL MY LOVE"
Great White could probably have made a career being any band they wanted to, and the fact that they chose to be themselves did more to delay the birth of tribute rock than any other of the reasons people should actually be ashamed for living someone else's good times. This time around, and all album long, a group that very appropriately named itself after an especially fearsome breed of shark chose to pick on Zeppelin, but not across just one song. They jabbed an entire album's worth of covers in our eyes. *Great Zeppelin*. Well, they got that bit right.

"THE BATTLE OF EVERMORE"
The Lovemongers were a Heart spin-off, whose self-titled debut album took a glorious nod back at the parent band's early daze with this almost-as-good-as-the-real-thing retread.

"BLACK DOG"

Zakk Wylde covered the classics (we know this, because that's what the album was titled). "Black Dog" was the best of the batch.

"BLACK MOUNTAIN SIDE"

Dread Zeppelin was a reggae band, a genre Zeppelin only ever glanced at once, with the jokily titled "D'yer Mak'er." That did not, however, stop Dread from making a career out of Led, and this cut from their first LP, *Un-Led-Ed*, will either convert you to their madness on the spot, or send you screaming from the room, in search of a priest.

"COMMUNICATION BREAKDOWN"

The Dickies were an L.A. punk band who specialized in light-speed reinterpretations of classic rock staples. "Nights in White Satin" and "Paranoid" both fell prey to their speedball dementia, and so did the theme to TV's *Banana Splits*. But if you ever wondered what Led Zeppelin would sound like if the entire band were breathing helium, this answers that question at the same time, remarkably, as losing none of the original's urgency.

"THE CRUNGE"

Gov't Mule, for reasons one can only guess at, rerecorded the entire *Houses of the Holy* album as *Haunted Holy House*, and sold it through their website. It's actually very good.

"CUSTARD PIE"

Helmet teamed with Jesus Lizard's David Yow to bring some good old nineties alterna-metal thrash to *Encomium*. They didn't really need to.

"D'YER MAK'ER"

Sheryl Crow had already won a Grammy, duetted with the Stones, sung backup for Michael Jackson, toured with Dylan, and headlined Woodstock '94 by the time she gifted *Encomium* with her take on Zeppelin's first and only stab at reggae. Also assaulted by Great White on *Great Zeppelin*.

"DANCING DAYS"

Stone Temple Pilots were one of the non-Seattle bands who rose up from the rest of America's attempts to grasp some grunge glory for itself. Hailing from Southern California, they were no better, no worse, than the rest, but if you pick up *Encomium*, you're stuck with them.

"DAZED AND CONFUSED"

Nirvana were still mere striplings rehearsing when they laid this down, and you've probably already gathered that this list is decidedly not dedicated to the best Zeppelin covers ever made. It's the ones you most need to hear, because *this* is how far the band's influence spread.

"DOWN BY THE SEASIDE"

Tori Amos would probably be better suited to a Kate Bush tribute than a Zeppelin one. But, teaming up with some guy named Robert Plant, she closed *Encomium* with a surprisingly effective take on …well, let's be honest about it. "Down by the Seaside" is *nobody's* favorite song from *Physical Graffiti*.

"FOOL IN THE RAIN"

O.A.R. cut this *In Through the Out Door* beauty for a B-side. Which was about what it deserved.

"FOUR STICKS"

The Rollins Band, led by the eponymous Henry, were the grinding hardcore metal alter ego of a performer who is just as well regarded for his writing, radio show, acting, and ability to combine all those into one of the best stand-up routines around. *Encomium* creaked beneath the weight of this one.

"FRIENDS"
Elliott Smith included a great live version of "Friends" in his 2001-ish live set, thankfully preserved on an accompanying live album.

"GOING TO CALIFORNIA"
Never the Bride were a brand-new, unheard, and untried band when they were invited onto *Encomium*. They remained so thereafter.

"GOOD TIMES BAD TIMES"
Cracker was the brainchild of former Camper Van Beethoven frontman David Lowery and, across two albums in the early to mid-1990s, emerged as one of the most enjoyable rock 'n' bluegrass, country-pop-alternative bands in America. Sadly never to escape the shadow of Lowery's past, they fizzled out in the end, but this gift to *Encomium* captures them in all their crooked-grinned glory.

"HEARTBREAKER"
Coalesce coalesced around the *Led Zeppelin II* stomper on their *There Is Nothing New under the Sun* album. And they were right. There isn't.

"HEY HEY WHAT CAN I DO"
Hootie & the Blowfish. South Carolina's most hideously named export had never made any secret of their early indebtedness to Zeppelin, although a throwaway 1971 B-side many fans never heard until it appeared on the *Led Zeppelin* box set probably wasn't the best showcase for such devotion. Another one for *Encomium*.

"HOTS ON FOR NOWHERE"
Van Halen had a handful of Zeppelin covers in their early live repertoire, with this one surviving long enough to be taped for the first *Live Anthology* compilation.

"IMMIGRANT SONG"
Trent Reznor and Karen O combine for what can only be described as the most scarifying movie theme of 2011, for *The Girl*

with the Dragon Tattoo. Highlights include a post-industrial throb that is genuinely exciting, metallic drums and monkish vocals that might not have been made by humans at all, and the fact that it takes both vocalists to re-create the range Plant found so easy. A magnificent rendering.

"KASHMIR"
The Dixie Dregs might have been locked in solid Southern-rock mode, but they stepped out of both character and geography for this sensational reading, from the *Bring 'Em Back Alive* CD.

"THE LEMON SONG"
The Black Crowes might be cheating, getting on this list with Jimmy Page on guitar. But it's a great version on an album that is all too frequently overlooked.

"MISTY MOUNTAIN HOP"
San Francisco's 4 Non Blondes wrapped up their career by re-cording one final song together, destined for the Zeppelin tribute album *Encomium.*

"MOBY DICK"
All That. From the fittingly titled *Whop Boom Bam* album…what a great idea! A cover version of a drum solo that was seldom played the same two nights running.

"NIGHT FLIGHT"
Jeff Buckley's version can be found on the 2003 extended release of his *Live at Sin-é* cafe recording.

"NO QUARTER"
Tool takes a song that will forever be enshrined as an excuse for John Paul Jones to go all supper club on our asses, and gives it a mean metal sheen instead.

"THE OCEAN"

Living Colour were a band many bad-tempered critics inexplicably adored in the very late 1980s, probably because their biggest hit, "Cult of Personality," sounded exactly like something bad-tempered critics liked to write, and was a self-fulfilling prophecy too. Hubris can be a real bitch sometimes. And in the meantime, a song like "The Ocean" would probably be nailed by the thought police before it ever got to radio today. *How* old did you say your little girl was?

"OUT ON THE TILES"

Blind Melon. The Almost Zeppelin of the early 1990s were a shoo-in for *Encomium*.

"RAMBLE ON"

One of a multitude of highlights on one of the most shockingly successful of all Zeppelin tributes, **Iron Horse**'s *The Bluegrass Tribute to…*

"ROCK AND ROLL"

Rasputina were one of those bands that were either the best idea ever (Cossack-sounding cellists from hell) or just another of those peculiar gimmicks to which rock is occasionally heir. This is probably the peak of their mad hybrid, and a joy to listen to, even today.

"SINCE I'VE BEEN LOVING YOU"

Europe warned us of the Final Countdown, but clearly we didn't take them seriously enough. Because they clung together for a long time thereafter, and this unsuspecting blues is numbered among their most hapless victims.

"SOUTH BOUND SAUREZ"

The Dead Milkmen not only had a great name, they had great taste in B-sides as well.

"STAIRWAY TO HEAVEN"

Pat Boone's conversion to heavy metal is another of those novelty nasties with which the nineties overflowed, although the fact it became his biggest album in decades probably wasn't indicative of a massive upsurge in America's capacity for ironic humor. What is worth noting, however, is that of several hundred versions of this song recorded over the decades, ranging from the triumphantly visionary (Heart) to the oddball-lunatic appealing (Rolf Harris), and on through every other emotion and humor you could hope for, this is one of the few that can be safely categorized as quietly competent.

"TANGERINE"

Big Head Todd and the Monsters had already toured with Robert Plant, and racked up three Top 10 singles on the AOR chart when they were invited to appear on *Encomium*. Which just goes to show ...

"TEN YEARS GONE"

Jason Bonham, son of John, has carved himself an excellent career that acknowledges but never seeks to capitalize on his father's old glories. Drafted into Zeppelin itself on the occasion of Atlantic Records' 40th anniversary celebration in 1994, he would pay tribute to Dad and Co. in 1997 with the aptly named *In the Name of My Father: The Zepset—Live from Electric Ladyland*. Ten Zeppelin classics come under the microscope (none of which were "Moby Dick" or "Bonzo's Montreux"), and this isn't even the best. But it is definitely one of them. All proceeds from the album, by the way, were donated to the John Bonham Memorial Motorcycle Camp and the Big Sisters of Los Angeles.

"THANK YOU"

Duran Duran emerged from Britain's early-1980s New Romantic movement, a primarily synth and haircut-led scene whose superficiality disguised a number of surprisingly enduring talents. Duran, who dominated the early 1980s like no other rock band of the age, were one of them, and *Encomium* was all the better for their presence.

"THAT'S THE WAY"

Gerald "Jezz" Woodroffe was Robert Plant's keyboard player through much of the early 1980s, cowriter of a handful of genuine Percy classics, and also the mastermind behind this smoky nightclub jewel. A collection titled *In Through the Swing Door: Swing Cover Versions of Led Zeppelin Classics* might not be everybody's idea of the ideal Christmas gift. But you'd be surprised what evocative fun it turns out to be.

"WHEN THE LEVEE BREAKS"

Kristin Hersh's *Strings* album is an oft-overlooked joy. And so is this.

"WHOLE LOTTA LOVE"

CCS was the legendary jazz-rock band fronted by the legendary blues-rock master Alexis Korner at the dawn of the 1970s. They laid claim to a couple of Zeppelin numbers, including a truly baying "Black Dog." But their greatest moment, and a U.K. hit single too, has to be this, an electrifying instrumental version of the *Led Zeppelin II* standout that became the theme to long-running U.K. pop TV show *Top of the Pops* for much of the 1970s.

APPENDIX B:
FORTY MUST-SEE TV AND MOVIE APPEARANCES

"ACHILLES LAST STAND"
British TV's *The Old Grey Whistle Test* announced the release of *Presence* by combining the LP track with some oddly effective, but wholly irrelevant library footage. A live version was filmed at Knebworth in August 1979 and included on the *Led Zeppelin* DVD. But this one is somehow more fitting.

"BABE I'M GONNA LEAVE YOU"
Filmed live for Danish TV's *TV Byen* on March 17, 1969 (broadcast on May 19). But of course, what we really want to see is the version shot for Germany's *Beat Club* ten days later.

"BLACK DOG"
Don Kirshner's Rock Concert described it as Zeppelin's first-ever U.S. TV appearance, although actually it was simply footage from *The Song Remains the Same*. Footage from the same Madison Square Garden shows in July 1973 was also included on the *Led Zeppelin* DVD.

"BRING IT ON HOME"
One more from the Royal Albert Hall, January 9, 1970.

"BRON-Y-AUR STOMP"
Filmed at Earls Court, London, in May 1975 and included on the *Led Zeppelin* DVD.

"C'MON EVERYBODY"

The Eddie Cochran cover was filmed at the Royal Albert Hall, January 9, 1970.

"COMMUNICATION BREAKDOWN"

Filmed on several occasions in the months before the band abandoned TV performances. The best, as any true collector will tell you, are those we have no chance of ever seeing. In the meantime, we will console ourselves with either another excerpt from the March 1969 Danish *TV Byen* broadcast, a Swedish TV lip sync from three days earlier, or the Royal Albert Hall show the following January. While dreaming of their last-minute appearance on the BBC's *How Late It Is* on March 21, or *Tous En Scène* in June.

"DAZED AND CONFUSED"

For a short version, either *TV Byen*, *Beat Club*, or the U.K. *Supershow* the following week. For a longer feast, *The Song Remains the Same*. But for the most controversial, the band's June 19, 1969, appearance on French television's *Tous En Scène* was the one that finally decided manager Peter Grant against allowing Zeppelin to appear on TV again.

"GOING TO CALIFORNIA"

Filmed at Earls Court, London, in May 1975 and included on the *Led Zeppelin* DVD.

"GOOD TIMES BAD TIMES"

Shot for Dutch television's *Jam TV* on March 29, 1969.

"HEARTBREAKER"

From *The Song Remains the Same*.

"HOW MANY MORE TIMES"

Shot for Danish TV's *TV Byen* on March 17, 1969, and broadcast on May 19. Or, one more from the Royal Albert Hall, January 9, 1970.

"I CAN'T QUIT YOU BABY"
One more from the Royal Albert Hall, January 9, 1970.

"IMMIGRANT SONG"
Merged with offstage footage for Dutch TV's *Hard Rock Heaven* on May 27, 1972. A version filmed in Sydney, Australia, on February 27, 1972, was included on the *Led Zeppelin* DVD.

"IN MY TIME OF DYING"
Filmed at Earls Court, London, in May 1975 and included on the *Led Zeppelin* DVD.

"IN THE EVENING"
Filmed at Knebworth in August 1979 and included on the *Led Zeppelin* DVD.

"KASHMIR"
Filmed at Knebworth in August 1979 and included on the *Led Zeppelin* DVD.

"LET'S HAVE A PARTY"
ABC's *Get to Know You* used some live footage of the song to accompany a John Bonham interview on February 27, 1972.

"LONG TALL SALLY"
The Little Richard cover is one more from the Royal Albert Hall, January 9, 1970.

"MISTY MOUNTAIN HOP"
Filmed at Madison Square Garden in July 1973, and included on the *Led Zeppelin* DVD.

"MOBY DICK"
Footage from *The Song Remains the Same* accompanied a British TV interview with John Bonham, broadcast on *All Right Now* on March 4, 1980. A decade earlier, the studio version of the same song was

employed as the theme to the show *Disco Now*. A stunning live take also features on the Royal Albert Hall film.

"NO QUARTER"

Zeppelin's prohibition on TV performance was no obstacle to British TV's *Old Grey Whistle Test*. They simply dug out library stock footage that seemed to fit the music and created some truly magical montages. Three years later, a live version rolled up on *The Song Remains the Same*.

"NOBODY'S FAULT BUT MINE"

Filmed at Knebworth in August 1979 and included on the *Led Zeppelin* DVD.

"THE OCEAN"

Filmed at Madison Square Garden in July 1973 and included on the *Led Zeppelin* DVD.

"OVER THE HILLS AND FAR AWAY"

Given a video once-over for the 1990 box set.

"THE RAIN SONG"

From *The Song Remains the Same*.

"ROCK AND ROLL"

The Song Remains the Same is the best version, but Live Aid is popular, simply because it has yet to be released. ABC's *Get to Know You* used some live footage of the song to accompany a John Bonham interview on February 27, 1972, and the *Led Zeppelin* DVD featured footage from Knebworth in August 1979. The same collection also includes a version from Sydney in 1972.

"SICK AGAIN"

Filmed at Knebworth in August 1979 and included on the *Led Zeppelin* DVD.

"SINCE I'VE BEEN LOVING YOU"
From *The Song Remains the Same*. Footage from the same Madison Square Garden shows in July 1973 was included on the *Led Zeppelin* DVD.

"SOMETHING ELSE"
One more from the Royal Albert Hall, January 9, 1970.

"THE SONG REMAINS THE SAME"
From *The Song Remains the Same*.

"STAIRWAY TO HEAVEN"
The Song Remains the Same packs a peerless rendition; Live Aid serves up an apostolic one. But the best was filmed at Earls Court, London, in May 1975 and included on the *Led Zeppelin* DVD.

"THAT'S THE WAY"
Filmed at Earls Court, London, in May 1975 and included on the *Led Zeppelin* DVD.

"TRAMPLED UNDER FOOT"
Is this Led Zeppelin's greatest TV performance? Broadcast February 21, 1975, an *Old Grey Whistle Test* special matched the newly released album track with some fabulous footage of old-time dancing girls, and it worked better than any "deliberate" music video could ever hope. A live performance was filmed at Earls Court, London, in May 1975 and included on the *Led Zeppelin* DVD, but quite frankly, it's drab compared to the Filmfinders footage, as a few minutes visiting YouTube will prove.

"TRAVELLING RIVERSIDE BLUES"
Recorded for radio broadcast at the BBC studios on June 24, 1969, and then transformed into an "official promo video" in 1990, for the release of the four-CD box set.

"WE'RE GONNA GROOVE"
One more from the Royal Albert Hall, January 9, 1970.

"WHAT IS AND WHAT SHOULD NEVER BE"
One more from the Royal Albert Hall, January 9, 1970.

"WHITE SUMMER"/"BLACK MOUNTAIN SIDE"
Recorded by Page alone as a guest on BBC TV's *Julie Felix Show* on April 23, 1970. They also appear in the film of the Royal Albert Hall show, January 9, 1970.

"WHOLE LOTTA LOVE"
One more from the Royal Albert Hall, January 9, 1970. Or *The Song Remains the Same*. Or Live Aid. Or Knebworth. Or, if you don't mind a really freaky psychedelic collage, interspersed with footage from the previous year's appearance on *Beat Club*, their next appearance on that show, on March 28, 1970. The studio version, meanwhile, was the theme music to British TV's *Search*. (The famous rendering that opened *Top of the Pops* was performed by CCS—see Appendix A.)

"YOU SHOOK ME"
From that elusive *Beat Club* performance on March 27, 1969.

APPENDIX C:
FURTHER READING AND WRITINGS

Hammer of the Gods: The Led Zeppelin Saga
By Stephen Davis
(IT BOOKS/HARPERCOLLINS, NEW YORK CITY, 2008)

The best Zep book there is (or, at least, the best-known), *Hammer of the Gods* is the happy collision of a very well-researched story, a very well-informed author and—as if we'd care if it weren't the case—a very gossip 'n' rumor–prone band. Drawing upon the revelations of a roomful of Zep friends/associates, the most controversial elements of *Hammer of the Gods* would be damped down somewhat by the subsequent appearance of Richard Cole's *Stairway to Heaven*, in which tales only alluded to here are spread out in all their gory glory.

But Davis—like Zeppelin themselves—came to do more than slide fish inside groupies. His understanding not only of their music, but also of what that music meant to the wider world of rock 'n' roll, carries the story even when its chief protagonists are otherwise occupied—it wasn't fun and games all the time, after all. Sometimes they even made records.

Similarly, his handling of the chain of tragedies that scarred the band's last years together draws upon the knowledge that one doesn't *have* to have sold one's soul to the Devil for bad things to occur. Sometimes, shit just happens. But the Satanic rumors are here, just in case, together with pretty much everything else you ever hoped you knew about the band. And if you don't think they were the cat's pajamas when you first pick up the book, by the end you'll be knitting puss a matching cap and dressing gown.

APPENDIX C

Stairway to Heaven—Led Zeppelin Uncensored
By Richard Cole and Richard Turbo
(IT BOOKS/HARPERCOLLINS, NEW YORK CITY, 2002)
Heard the one about four musicians, three groupies, and a bevy of horny wildebeest? Neither has Richard Cole. But, if it had happened (and one wouldn't be surprised), Zeppelin's incorrigible road manager would know all about it. Heck, he'd probably have arranged it. However, he can tell you what it's like to be bombarded with baked beans while screwing in front of a drummer, and he's watched ladies take the band in hand/mouth/ear/wherever while waiting for the solos to end.

Scorchingly scurrilous, and occasionally kinda scary, *Stairway* is the sort of book every band wishes could be written about them. But few could actually be proud if one were.

Led Zeppelin: The Definitive Biography
By Ritchie Yorke
(VIRGIN BOOKS, LONDON, 1993)
Originally published in 1974 (Sphere Books) at the height of Zeppelin's fame-so-far, *The Definitive Biography* would have been better served had this reprint simply been retitled "the first biography." Certainly the next decade or so of Zep biographing would have been a lot slimmer without it, but the work of subsequent writers (Cole, Davis, and Welch among them) so eclipses its contents that one wonders why rock fans even bothered learning to read back then. The 1993 update does expand the tale into the post-Zep era, but the book's main function today is to remind us how Zeppelin were viewed yesterday.

Led Zeppelin Live: An Illustrated Explanation of Underground Tapes
By Luis Rey
(COLLECTORS GUIDE PUBLISHING, TORONTO, CANADA, 1994)
Led Zeppelin have been described as the most bootlegged British rock band of the 1970s, and Luis Rey is ready to prove it. Detailing and describing more than 250 Zep concerts known to

circulate in underground circles, *Led Zeppelin Live* is either an insane accumulation of infuriating minutiae (who cares how long "Black Dog" went on for, that night in Santa Fe?), or the ultimate guide to the some of the greatest music you're not supposed to be listening to. Heftily, if not always brilliantly, illustrated with photos culled from sundry private collections, *Led Zeppelin Live* is a priceless road map to the bootleg jungle.

Led Zeppelin: The Concert File
By Dave Lewis and Simon Pallett
(OMNIBUS PRESS, LONDON, 2005)
And this is what that jungle would look like without it. Following the format of similar offerings on the Who and Hendrix, *The Concert File* is a date- and data-nut's paradise, a rabbit warren of circumstance and detail, pursuing Zeppelin from their first Scandinavian club dates to their farewell at Knebworth—and beyond, on both sides. A remarkable piece of work, in that the actual gigs form only the tip of the informational iceberg. The ability to chase a band around the world without once leaving the lavatory seat is one you never know you need until it's actually in your hand.

LZ-'75: The Lost Chronicles of Led Zeppelin's 1975 American Tour
By Stephen Davis
(GOTHAM BOOKS, NEW YORK CITY, 2010)
Half diary, half hindsight, the introduction explains how this is the story that didn't make Davis's *Hammer of the Gods* book, by virtue of the fact that he'd misplaced the notes. The main attraction probably didn't lose much by their omission, but as a stand-alone adjunct, this is a lot of fun. Less compulsive than, say, the published diaries from Bob Dylan's near-simultaneous Rolling Thunder tour (as produced by Larry Sloman and Sam Shepard), it is nevertheless an enjoyable insider's view of what made a tour like this tick, with added weight in the form of show reviews that do not pull punches.

Jimmy Page: Tangents Within a Framework
By Howard Mylett
(OMNIBUS PRESS, LONDON, 1984)
It's surprising, given the extent of Zep's fame, how few books delve into the lives of the individual members, as opposed to their conjoined existence as a leviathan. The Bonham book below is joined by just two more, Michael Gross's drab mid-seventies *Robert Plant*, and serial Zep scribe Mylett's rather more colorful *Tangents*—ninety-six pages of microprint and pictures that skip over the juicier elements of the guitarist's life, to document his day job. A discographical stab at sorting out the wealth of pre-Zep sessions remains useful despite subsequent research and revelations, while the enormity of the band's fame and achievements is conveyed with barrelhouse enthusiasm.

Treasures of Led Zeppelin
By Chris Welch
(CARLTON BOOKS, LONDON, 2010)
A glorious heavyweight packed to bursting with facsimile souvenirs of Led Zeppelin memorabilia. Think "pop-up book for grown-up readers," and smile as you pore over the fragile bits and pieces of someone else's scrapbook.

Led Zeppelin: Heaven and Hell
By Charles R. Cross and Erik Flannigan
(SIDGWICK & JACKSON, NEW YORK CITY, 1991)
The text is little more than an adequate reminder that the story remains the same—it's Neal Preston's spectacular photographs that make *Heaven and Hell* a true must-have. Interspersed between chapters that might have functioned better as articles in a well-dressed Zep fanzine, documenting the band's influences, collectibles, and a song-by-song synopsis, the pics not only capture some classic poses, they also double as a visual history of American metal throughout the last two decades: "Okay, if I put one leg up on the monitor, and throw my hair back like that, I'll look just like John Paul Jones." You see it *all the time*.

John Bonham: A Thunder of Drums
By Chris Welch and Geoff Nicholls
(BACKBEAT BOOKS, NEW YORK, 2001)
He drank! He drummed! He drank some more! Biographer Welch and drummer Nicholls combine for an anecdote-strewn rampage through the life of a musician, Welch remarks, whose "deep rumbling roar ... almost seemed to emanate from the bowels of the earth." And that was only in the bar. But who could not adore a man whose idea of fun was to mummify record company execs in sticky tape, then deposit them in the middle of Oxford Street? With appendices detailing Bonham's drum kits, and a track-by-track summary of his finest recorded moments, an affectionately, informatively, riotous read is spoiled only by the absence of a happy ending. He drummed! He drank! He died.

The Making of Led Zeppelin's IV
By Robert Godwin
(COLLECTORS GUIDE PUBLISHING, TORONTO, 2008)
The greatest album of the 1970s? Or the most overrated cack since *Sgt. Pepper?* You can choose, but before you do, seventy-two pages of *The Making of Led Zeppelin's IV* will ensure you make an informed choice. Part of a CD-size series that includes similar glimpses into albums by the Cure, U2 and, indeed, *Sgt. Pepper*, *The Making of* details everything from the construction of "Stairway to Heaven" through to the mystifying symbols that hang on the front cover. We still don't know what that bustle was doing in the hedgerow, but that's about the only question left unanswered.

Peter Grant: The Man Who Led Zeppelin
By Chris Welch
(OMNIBUS PRESS, LONDON, 2003)
The role of the rock 'n' roll manager has never been clearly defined. From nursemaiding reluctant crybabies to draining the blood from recalcitrant promoters, there are few tasks the average Mr. Fixit has not been called upon to do. And Peter Grant did most of them first. A gallivanting saga that traces Grant from his days as an all-in

wrestler, through his muscular presence on the sixties club scene, and on to his decade-plus spent inflating the Zeppelin, *The Man Who* cuts through the impenetrable veil of fearful silence that once surrounded Grant's doings, to portray a man of such ferocious loyalty that there was nothing he wouldn't have done for his boys. Seriously, *nothing*.

Led Zeppelin ... The Press Reports
By Robert Godwin
(COLLECTORS GUIDE PUBLISHING, TORONTO, 1997)
Remember back in your first flush of pop-loving youth, the scrapbooks you so assiduously created, of every mention the papers ever made of your heroes? And remember how you eventually tired of them, and wound up dumping them the last time you moved? Robert Godwin does. What's more, he feels your pain. Arranged chronologically, more than a thousand vintage Zeppress cuttings tell the tale as it happened at the time, in the language of the age. Sadly for true nostalgics, the ink won't come off on your fingers; but if you need to know what *Circus* thought about *The Song Remains the Same* (and, of course, you do), this is where to turn.

Dazed and Confused: The Stories Behind Every Song
By Chris Welch
(CARLTON BOOKS, LONDON, 1998)
Zeppelin were not the most reactive of songwriters. Little of their oeuvre actually sprang from direct personal experience, while the best hidden meanings tended to be mere double entendres. Squeeze my lemon, indeed. The tales of contested ownership—and there's a whole lotta them—are intriguing, but the book's greatest strength lies in refocusing familiar aspects of the Zeppelin story to the songs and sessions that they applied to, as opposed to blurring past amid a sea of accomplishments. Which, in turns, leaves you wanting to actually listen to the records, as opposed to simply playing them.

APPENDIX D:
HOWLING THE ODDS: ONE HUNDRED MUST-HAVE ALBUMS

1. Bad Company: *Bad Company* (Swan Song 1974)
2. Bad Company: *Straight Shooter* (Swan Song 1975)
3. Jeff Beck Group: *Beck-Ola* (Epic 1969)
4. Jeff Beck Group: *Truth* (Epic 1968)
5. Maggie Bell: *Queen of the Night* (Atlantic 1974)
6. Maggie Bell: *Suicide Sal* (Swan Song 1975)
7. Chuck Berry: *The Chess Box* (box set) (Chess 1988)
8. Black Crowes: *Amorica* (Def American 1994)
9. Black Crowes: *Shake Your Money Maker* (Def American 1990)
10. Black Crowes: *The Southern Harmony and Musical Companion* (Def American 1992)
11. Black Crowes: *Three Snakes and One Charm* (Def American 1996)
12. Black Sabbath: *Black Sabbath* (Warner Brothers 1970)
13. Black Sabbath: *Paranoid* (Warner Brothers 1970)
14. Blind Melon: *Blind Melon* (Capitol 1992)
15. Cream: *Disraeli Gears* (Atco 1967)
16. Cream: *Fresh Cream* (Atco 1967)
17. Cream: *Wheels of Fire* (Atco 1968)
18. Deep Purple: *In Rock* (Warner Brothers 1970)
19. Keith De Groot: *No Introduction Necessary* (Spark 1969)
20. Sandy Denny: *Who Knows Where the Time Goes?* (box set) (Island 1985)
21. Bo Diddley: *The Chess Box* (box set) (Chess 1990)

22. Willie Dixon: *The Chess Box* (box set) (Chess 1988)
23. Donovan: *Hurdy Gurdy Man* (Epic 1968)
24. Donovan: *Mellow Yellow* (Epic 1967)
25. Donovan: *Sunshine Superman* (Epic 1966)
26. Fairport Convention: *Heyday* (compilation)
27. Fairport Convention: *Liege and Lief* (A&M 1969)
28. Fairport Convention: *Unhalfbricking* (A&M 1969)
29. Fairport Convention: *What We Did on Our Holidays*
    (A&M 1969)
30. Marianne Faithfull: *North Country Maid* (London 1966)
31. Fleetwood Mac: *Mr. Wonderful* (Blue Horizon 1968)
32. Fleetwood Mac: *Peter Green's Fleetwood Mac*
    (Blue Horizon 1967)
33. Free: *Fire and Water* (A&M 1970)
34. Free: *Free* (A&M 1969)
35. Free: *Tons of Sobs* (A&M 1969)
36. Rory Gallagher: *Deuce* (Polydor 1971)
37. Rory Gallagher: *Rory Gallagher* (Polydor 1971)
38. Rory Gallagher: *Tattoo* (Polydor 1973)
39. Graham Gouldman: *The Graham Gouldman Thing*
    (RCA 1968)
40. Roy Harper: *Bullinamingvase* (Harvest 1977)
41. Roy Harper: *Folkjokeopus* (Harvest 1969)
42. Roy Harper: *Stormcock* (Harvest 1971)
43. Roy Harper: *Whatever Happened to Jugula?*
    (Beggars Banquet 1985)
44. Heart: *Zeppish* (Sony 2012)
45. Heart: *Dreamboat Annie* (Capitol 1976)
46. Heart: *Little Queen* (Portrait 1977)
47. Jimi Hendrix Experience: *Electric Ladyland* (Reprise 1968)
48. Herman's Hermits & Peter Noone: *Into Something Good*
    (box set) (EMI 2008)
49. Son House: *Martin Scorsese Presents the Blues* (compilation)
    (Sony 2004)
50. Howlin' Wolf: *The Chess Box* (box set) (Chess 1991)

51. Howlin' Wolf: *The London Howlin' Wolf Sessions* (Chess 1991)
52. J.B. Lenoir: *Martin Scorsese Presents the Blues* (compilation) (Sony 2004)
53. John Mayall: *A Hard Road* (London 1967)
54. John Mayall: *Blues Alone* (London 1967)
55. John Mayall: *Blues Breakers with Eric Clapton* (London 1966)
56. John Mayall: *Crusade* (London 1967)
57. John Mayall: *Plays John Mayall* (Decca 1965)
58. Robert Johnson: *Martin Scorsese Presents the Blues* (compilation) (Sony 2004)
59. Robert Johnson: *The Complete Original Masters: Centennial Edition* (box set) (Sony 2011)
60. B.B. King: *Martin Scorsese Presents the Blues* (compilation) (Sony 2004)
61. Kingdom Come: *This Is Kingdom Come* (Polydor 1988)
62. The Mission: *Children* (Mercury 1988)
63. Nazareth: *Loud 'n' Proud* (A&M 1973)
64. Nazareth: *Razamanaz* (A&M 1973)
65. Pink Floyd: *The Piper at the Gates of Dawn* (Tower 1967)
66. Queen: *Queen I* (Elektra 1973)
67. Queen: *Queen II* (Elektra 1974)
68. Queen: *Sheer Heart Attack* (Elektra 1974)
69. Otis Redding: *Otis! The Definitive Otis Redding* (box set) (Rhino 1973)
70. Cliff Richard: *The Rock 'n' Roll Years* (box set) (EMI 1997)
71. Rolling Stones: *Beggars Banquet* (London 1968)
72. Rolling Stones: *Let It Bleed* (London 1969)
73. Shadows: *Complete Singles As & Bs* (box set) (EMI 2006)
74. Bessie Smith: *Martin Scorsese Presents the Blues* (compilation) (Sony 2004)
75. Soundgarden: *Superunknown* (A&M 1994)
76. Al Stewart: *Love Chronicles* (CBS 1969)
77. Stone the Crows: *Ode to John Law* (Polydor 1970)

78. Stone the Crows: *Stone the Crows* (Polydor 1970)
79. Screaming Lord Sutch: *Rock and Horror* (Ace 2004)
80. Vanilla Fudge: *Vanilla Fudge* (Atco 1967)
81. Various artists: *Martin Scorsese Presents the Blues: Godfathers and Sons* (Sony 2004)
82. Various artists: *Martin Scorsese Presents the Blues: Feel Like Going Home* (Sony 2004)
83. Various artists: *Martin Scorsese Presents the Blues: Piano Blues* (Sony 2004)
84. Various artists: *Martin Scorsese Presents the Blues: Red, White & Blues* (Sony 2004)
85. Various artists: *Martin Scorsese Presents the Blues: The Road to Memphis* (Sony 2004)
86. Various artists: *Martin Scorsese Presents the Blues: The Soul of a Man* (Sony 2004)
87. Various artists: *Martin Scorsese Presents the Blues: Warming by the Devil's Fire* (Sony 2004)
88. Stevie Ray Vaughan: *Martin Scorsese Presents the Blues* (compilation) (Sony 2004)
89. Gene Vincent: *Complete Capitol and Columbia Recordings* (box set) (EMI 1990)
90. Muddy Waters: *Martin Scorsese Presents the Blues* (compilation) (Sony 2004)
91. Jack White: *Blunderbuss* (Sony 2012)
92. White Stripes: *De Stijl* (Warner Brothers 2000)
93. White Stripes: *White Blood Cells* (Warner Brothers 2001)
94. Sonny Boy Williamson: *And the Yardbirds* (Mercury 1966)
95. Sonny Boy Williamson: *Don't Send Me No Flowers* (Marmalade 1968)
96. Yardbirds: *For Your Love* (Epic 1965)
97. Yardbirds: *Having a Rave Up* (Epic 1965)
98. Yardbirds: *Little Games* (Epic 1967)
99. Yardbirds: *Live Yardbirds! Featuring Jimmy Page* (Epic 1971)
100. Yardbirds: *Roger the Engineer* (Columbia 1966)

INDEX

INDEX

Blackmore, Ritchie, 66, 116, 132
Blind Faith, 37, 97
Blind Melon, 144, 162
Blue Cheer, 10
Bonham, Jason, 120, 153, 163
Bono, 2
Boone, Pat, 163
Bowie, David, 15, 71, 105,
 106, 111, 112, 113
Box of Frogs, 49
Bredon, Anne, 28, 29
Brian Howard and the
 Silhouettes, 53
"Bring It On Home," 21, 165
"Bron-Y-Aur Stomp," 165
Broonzy, Big Bill, 91
Brown, Roy, 118
Bruce, Jack, 20, 129
Buckley, Jeff, 161
Budgie, 140
Byrds, the, 14, 38, 55

Canned Heat, 91
Carolina Chocolate Drops, 20
Carter-Lewis and the
 Southerners, 53
Carthy, Eliza, 69
CCS, 164
Charlton, Manny, 99
Chicken Shack, 90
Clapton, Eric, 33, 34, 36–37,
 39, 62, 63, 86, 87, 91, 93,
 112, 129, 149
Coalesce, 160
Cochran, Eddie, 10, 64, 110,
 166

Cocker, Joe, 65, 91
Coda, 21
"Communication Breakdown,"
 158, 166
Cracker, 160
Crazy World of Arthur Brown,
 the, 14, 78, 91
Cream, 6, 8, 11–12, 22, 37, 41,
 86, 88, 90, 91, 93, 96, 129
Crow, Sheryl, 158
Crowley, Aleister, 24–25
Crudup, Arthur "Big Boy," 23
"Crunge, The," 158
Cult, the, 142, 145
Current 93, 69
"Custard Pie," 158

Daltrey, Roger, 40
"Dancing Days," 159
Davies, Cyril, 20
Davies, Dave, 38, 54
Davies, Ray, 13, 54
"Dazed and Confused," 30–31,
 151, 159, 166
Dead Milkmen, 162
Deep Purple, 2, 103, 120, 132,
 140, 141
Def Leppard, 140
De Groot, Keith, 49, 64
Denny, Sandy, 71, 72, 77–82
Des Barres, Michael, 104
DeShannon, Jackie, 55
Detective, 104
Diamond Head, 140
Dickies, the, 139, 158
Diddley, Bo, 22, 105

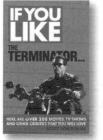